COUNTRY
FLAVORS

60 Years
of
Great Home Cooking

By Marion Seguin

Front Cover

Standing Rib Roast, page 112
Roast Potatoes, page 82
Mom's Baked Beans, page 75

COUNTRY FLAVORS
by
Marion Seguin

First Printing — August 1993

Published by
Bakers Trading Inc.
R.R. #2
Stony Plain, Alberta
Canada, T0E 2G0

Canadian Cataloguing in Publication Data

Seguin, Marion, 1919 —

   Country flavors

   Includes index.
   ISBN 1-895292-26-3

1. Cookery.   I. Title.

TX714.S44 1993   641.5   C93-098133-2

Photography by:
Merle Prosofsky
Merle Prosofsky Photography
Edmonton, Alberta

Dishes and Accessories Compliments of:
Eaton's

Designed, Printed and Produced in Canada by:
Centax Books, a Division of PrintWest Communications Ltd.
Publishing Director, Photo Designer & Food Stylist: Margo Embury
1150 Eighth Avenue, Regina, Saskatchewan, Canada S4R 1C9
(306) 525-2304   FAX: (306) 757-2439

TABLE OF CONTENTS

Recipes have been tested in U.S. Standard measurements. Common metric measurements are given as a convenience for those who are more familiar with metric. Recipes have not been tested in metric.

INTRODUCTION

From the time I was twelve years old, baking and cooking have been the joy of my life. Today I still love to cook and entertain, especially for my sons, Ray and Jack, and my five grandchildren and their friends. They and many of my friends have encouraged me to write this cookbook and share my family recipes. In the Ukrainian culture I grew up in and the French Canadian culture of my husband's family, sharing food and hospitality were part of sharing our culture. During my sixty years of cooking I have shared recipes with friends from many ethnic backgrounds. I also love to experiment with and develop new recipes. **Country Flavors** *is the result of my lifelong enjoyment of cooking.*

I was raised on a farm near Bellis, Alberta, a very small town northeast of Edmonton. We had to depend on our family and neighbors for companionship and entertainment. The people there were warm and friendly. There was a wonderful sense of community and, of course, good food played an important part in every gathering.

Growing up on a farm, we used all of our own produce and we ate what was in season. Fresh Vegetable Borscht was a summer soup that featured fresh garden vegetables. Ukrainian Borscht was a winter soup that was traditionally made to use up the beets in the root cellar. We raised our own chickens and before we could cook Chicken in Cream we had to catch the chickens then run to the well to bring up the cream from cold storage.

When I married into a French Canadian family, my cooking embraced all of the wonderful flavors of traditional French Canadian cooking. My husband, Anselme Seguin and I lived on a farm at Bonneville, Alberta for many years. We raised chickens, pigs and cows, and I had a large vegetable garden. My children enjoyed both the Ukrainian and French dishes. My husband loved desserts and sweets. Special favorites were Sucre à Créme and pies of any kind, served with rich farm cream, of course.

Both of my sons have inherited my appreciation and passion for good food. My son, Ray, has been involved in catering businesses in Alberta and has fed many thousands of people with his special steaks and combination Prime Rib and Bar-B-Q Whole Red Spring Salmon. Over 50,000 #1 T-bone steaks were served annually at Little Acres Bar-B-Q in Winterburn.

Cookies were always a special part of my baking. My children, grandchildren and many others paid me the practical compliment of regularly emptying my cookie jar. My Chocolate Chip cookies were especially favored and in 1984 my son, Jack, founded English Bay Batter in Vancouver, featuring "Grandma Marion's scrumptious chocolate chip cookie dough". Many flavors of English Bay Cookie Batter are now marketed across North America to grocery chains, restaurants and in major fund-raising campaigns for schools, community, sports and charitable organizations.

*This book is the result of over sixty years of cooking for family and friends. It is a combination of the best of many cultures and traditions. I hope you enjoy the food and the spirit of **Country Flavors.***

Marion Seguin

DEDICATION

I dedicate this book to the

memory of my husband Anselme Seguin,

to my sons, Ray & Jack,

&

to my grandchildren,

Jacqueline, Stephen, Rochelle, Ryan & Jason.

COUNTRY
FLAVORS

Breakfast,
Brunch
&
Lunch

BUTTERMILK PANCAKES

Serve these fluffy pancakes plain or try one of the fruit or corn variations.

1½ cups	all-purpose flour	375 mL
1 tsp.	baking powder	2 mL
½ tsp.	baking soda	2 mL
2 tbsp.	sugar	30 mL
1 tsp.	salt	5 mL
2	eggs	2
2 cups	buttermilk	500 mL
½ cup	vegetable oil	125 mL
2 tbsp.		30 mL

Mix together dry ingredients. In another bowl, beat eggs, buttermilk and oil. Add to dry ingredients. Mix gently; don't overmix. Lightly grease a frying pan and, when hot, pour a large spoonful of batter for each pancake. When pancakes start to bubble, turn over and cook until light brown. Serve with your favorite syrup or jam. **Makes 15 pancakes.**

VARIATIONS: For Blueberry Pancakes, add 1 cup (250 mL) fresh or frozen blueberries to batter and stir lightly. Kernel corn, chopped apples or peaches may be substituted for the blueberries.

COTTAGE CHEESE PANCAKES

These make a very nice lunch dish, especially with sour cream and fresh fruit or you could serve them with sausages.

3	eggs	3
1 cup	cottage cheese	250 mL
¾ cup	flour	175 mL
¼ tsp.	salt	1 mL
4 tbsp.	melted butter or margarine	60 mL

Beat eggs, add remaining ingredients. Brush a frying pan with butter and cook as Buttermilk Pancakes, see above. **Serves 2.**

CHEESE NALYSNYKY

This Ukrainian blintz or crêpe recipe was given to me by a good friend. The casserole method makes them moist and tender.

3	eggs, beaten	3
1¼ cups	milk	300 mL
½ cup	melted butter or margarine	125 mL
¼ tsp.	salt	1 mL
1 cup	flour	250 mL

FILLING:

3 cups	dry cottage cheese	750 mL
½ cup	fresh bread crumbs	125 mL
1	egg	1
½ tsp.	salt	2 mL
dash	pepper	dash
1 tsp.	sugar	5 mL
1 tbsp.	butter	15 mL
½ cup	whipping cream	125 mL

Combine first 4 ingredients. Add flour; beat until blended. Set aside. To make filling, put cottage cheese in a blender or food processor and process until smooth. Add bread crumbs, egg, salt, pepper and sugar and mix well. Heat an oiled 6" (15 cm) skillet. Put 2 tbsp. (30 mL) of batter in skillet and cook on 1 side. Remove pancake to plate, put a tablespoon (15 mL) of cheese filling on uncooked side and fold in the sides and the ends; place in 2, 2-quart (2 L) casseroles. Repeat with remaining batter and filling. When casserole is filled, dot with butter and top with whipping cream. Bake at 350°F (180°C) for 30-40 minutes, until cream bubbles. Serve with sour cream. **Serves 10-12.**

VARIATION: Fry filled blintzes in butter and serve with sour cream.

See photograph on page 87.

WAFFLES

2	eggs	2
2 cups	flour	500 mL
½ cup	margarine, butter or oil	125 mL
1¾ cups	milk	425 mL
1 tbsp.	sugar	15 mL
4 tsp.	baking powder	20 mL
½ tsp.	salt	2 mL

Heat waffle iron. Beat eggs until fluffy; add the rest of the ingredients and beat until smooth. Pour ½ cup (125 mL) of batter into the middle of the hot iron. Bake until steaming stops, about 4-5 minutes. Remove waffle carefully. Serve with butter and your favorite syrup. **Serves 4-6.**

FRENCH TOAST

5	eggs	5
¼ cup	creamilk (10% m.f.)	60 mL
1 tbsp.	sugar	15 mL
¼ tsp.	salt	1 mL
8	thick slices of French bread with crust	8
4 tbsp.	butter	60 mL
	syrup, jam or icing sugar	

Beat together eggs, cream, sugar and salt. Dip slices of bread into egg mixture and fry in butter. Cook for 4-5 minutes on each side. Keep hot in oven until ready to serve with your favorite syrup or jam or sprinkle with icing sugar. **Serves 4.**

CORN OR FRUIT FRITTERS

My son, Ray, loves these delicious fritters.

1¾ cups	flour	425 mL
1 tbsp.	baking powder	15 mL
1 tbsp.	sugar	15 mL
½ tsp.	salt	2 mL
2	eggs, beaten	2
1 cup	milk	250 mL
1 tbsp.	melted butter or margarine	15 mL
1-2 cups	corn or berries or chopped fruit	250-500 mL

Sift together dry ingredients. Combine eggs, milk and melted butter. Add to flour mixture and stir just to combine. If you are using the batter for corn, add 1-2 cups (250-500 mL) drained kernel corn. Drop batter by spoonfuls into hot oil or hot lard (365°F [185°F]). Don't make the fritters too big. Turn the fritters as soon as they brown on one side. Drain on paper towels. Keep fritters hot in oven. If making fruit fritters, add fruit instead of corn. Blueberries, chopped apples or peaches are tasty additions. Serve hot corn fritters with maple syrup. Dust fruit fritters with icing sugar. **Serves 8.**

BREAKFAST CASSEROLE

1 lb.	bulk sausage	500 g
6	eggs	6
2 cups	milk	500 mL
1 tsp.	salt	5 mL
	pepper to taste	
1 tsp.	dry mustard	5 mL
6	slices bread, crusts removed	6
1 cup	grated sharp cheese	250 mL

Sauté sausage and drain. Beat eggs with milk, salt, pepper and dry mustard. Place bread on bottom of greased 9 x 13" (22 x 33 cm) pan. Crumble sausage over bread and pour egg mixture on top. Refrigerate for 2-3 hours or overnight. Top with cheese. Bake at 350°F (180°C) for 40-50 minutes. Serve hot. **Serves 8.**

FRENCH OMELET

3-4	eggs	3-4
1 tbsp.	cold water	15 mL
$\frac{1}{4}$ tsp.	salt	1 mL
	pepper to taste	
1 tbsp.	butter	15 mL

Break eggs into a bowl. Add water, salt, pepper. Beat with a wire whisk just enough to mix the egg yolks and whites. In a 7" (18 cm) frying pan, heat the butter, tilting pan to grease entire bottom. Pour eggs in all at once. When eggs begin to set around the edges, lift omelet edges with a spatula, letting some of the egg mixture run underneath. When omelet is done but still moist on top, fold it in half and slide onto a warm plate. Serve immediately. **Serves 2.**

FILLING FOR OMELET: If you wish, fill with $\frac{1}{2}$ cup (125 mL) chopped ham, $\frac{1}{2}$ cup (125 mL) grated cheese or 2 green onions, finely chopped. Sprinkle over the eggs when the omelet is partially cooked.

PUFFY OMELET

4	eggs, separated	4
1/4 tsp.	cream of tartar	1 mL
1/4 tsp.	salt	1 mL
1/4 cup	cold water	60 mL
2 tbsp.	butter	30 mL

Preheat oven to 350°F (180°C). In a large bowl, beat egg whites until frothy. Add cream of tartar and beat until stiff peaks form. In a small bowl, beat egg yolks with salt and water until light and fluffy. Fold beaten egg whites into the egg yolk mixture. Use a frying pan that you can put in the oven. Heat frying pan on top of stove to melt butter. When butter is hot, pour in egg mixture. As omelet cooks, carefully lift around edges with spatula. When omelet is still runny, about half done, place frying pan in the oven for 10-15 minutes. Serve immediately. **Serves 2.**

VARIATION: You can sprinkle your favorite grated cheese on top of the omelet before putting it in the oven.

QUICHE

Use your favorite cheese to vary this quick and delicious quiche.

1	10" (25 cm) pie shell	1
1	egg white	1
1/2 lb.	bacon, cooked and crumbled	250 g
1 cup	grated Cheddar or Swiss cheese	250 mL
4	eggs, beaten	4
1 tbsp.	flour	15 mL
1 cup	creamilk (10% m.f.)	250 mL
1 cup	milk	250 mL
1/2 tsp.	salt	2 mL
1/4 tsp.	pepper	1 mL
3 or 4	green onions, chopped	3 or 4
2 tbsp.	butter	30 mL

Brush pie crust with egg white before baking, to prevent the crust from getting soggy. Bake pie crust for 10 minutes at 350°F (180°C). Spread bacon and cheese evenly over pie shell. Beat together eggs, flour, cream, milk, salt and pepper. Stir in green onions. Pour into pastry shell. Dot with small pieces of butter. Bake at 350°F (180°C) for 45-55 minutes. Serve with your favorite salad. **Serves 4-6.**

SPINACH AND MUSHROOM QUICHE

	pastry for 9" (23 cm) pie shell	
1	egg	1
1 tbsp.	water	15 mL
10 oz.	frozen chopped spinach	300 g
1 cup	chopped mushrooms	250 mL
2 tbsp.	butter	30 mL
½ lb.	Swiss or Cheddar cheese, grated	250 g
4	eggs	4
1 cup	whipping cream	250 mL
1 cup	milk	250 mL
1 tsp.	salt	5 mL
⅛ tsp.	pepper	0.5 mL

Line a quiche pan with pastry. Beat egg with water and brush the bottom and sides of the pastry shell. Bake crust for 10 minutes at 350°F (180°C). Remove from oven and prepare filling. Cook spinach for 10 minutes, drain and squeeze dry. In a skillet, sauté mushrooms in butter. Set aside. Sprinkle bottom of crust with half the cheese; cover with spinach and mushrooms, then the remaining cheese. In a bowl, beat 4 eggs, add cream and milk, salt and pepper. Pour egg mixture over cheese and bake quiche for 50-60 minutes at 350°F (180°C). Serve with a salad. **Serves 6.**

NOTE: 2 cups (500 mL) creamilk (10% m.f.) may be used instead of whipping cream and milk.

ZUCCHINI QUICHE

	pastry for 10" (25 cm) pie shell	
1	medium onion, finely chopped	1
1 tbsp.	butter or margarine	15 mL
4	eggs, well-beaten	4
1½ cups	creamilk (10% m.f.)	375 mL
1 tsp.	salt	5 mL
¼ tsp.	pepper	1 mL
2 cups	peeled, grated zucchini	500 mL
1 cup	grated Cheddar cheese	250 mL
1 tbsp.	flour	15 mL

Bake shell for 10 minutes at 400°F (200°C). Sauté onion in butter, set aside. Beat eggs with cream, salt and pepper; add grated zucchini, onions, grated cheese and flour. Pour into prepared pie shell. Bake at 350°F (180°C) for 50 to 60 minutes. Test with a knife in center of quiche. If knife comes out clean it is done. **Serves 6.**

GOLDEN CHEESE WHEEL

This is great to take on a picnic. It is like a covered pizza, filled with ham and cheese.

CRUST:

1 tbsp.	dry yeast (1 env.)	15 mL
1 tsp.	sugar	5 mL
1 cup	warm water	250 mL
2 cups	flour, or more if needed	500 mL
2 tbsp.	vegetable oil	30 mL
1 tsp.	salt	5 mL
1 tsp.	butter	5 mL

FILLING:

2	medium eggs, beaten	2
2 cups	grated Cheddar cheese, or other cheese	500 mL
2 tbsp.	dried parsley	30 mL
2	garlic cloves, grated	2
	pepper to taste	
1-2 cups	cubed ham, or more, or cooked sausage cut into pieces	250-500 mL
½ lb.	bacon, chopped, fried crisp, drained	250 g

EGG WASH:

1	egg, beaten	1
1 tsp.	water	5 mL
1 tbsp.	sesame seeds (optional)	15 mL

In a bowl, combine yeast, sugar and warm water. Let rest 5-8 minutes. Add 1 cup (250 mL) flour, oil, salt and mix well. Add remaining flour and knead for 3-4 minutes. Butter dough, cover and let rise until doubled in bulk, about 1 hour. Knead dough down and divide into 2. Let rest for 15 minutes. Roll half of dough into a 12" (30 cm) circle and place on cookie sheet. Combine all filling ingredients and spread evenly over dough, to within 1" (2.5 cm) of edge. Roll out the second piece of dough and place on top of cheese mixture. Brush edges with egg wash and seal. Cut slits in top crust for steam to escape. Brush with egg wash. Bake at 375°F (190°F) for 30 minutes. Remove from oven, brush top with egg wash and sprinkle with sesame seeds. Bake for 10 more minutes. Serve hot. It is also delicious cold. You can make the circles small and cut in wedges for snacks. Try using your regular bread dough for the crust. **Serves 8.**

VARIATION: Make 2 small wheels and cut in small wedges for appetizers. Use fried, drained sausage instead of ham.

See photograph on page 17.

COUNTRY
FLAVORS

Biscuits,
Muffins,
Loaves
&
Breads

BAKING POWDER BISCUITS

These are lovely light biscuits, perfect for strawberry shortcake. I got this recipe when I was in Paris, France.

2 cups	all-purpose flour	500 mL
1 tbsp.	baking powder	15 mL
2 tsp.	white sugar	10 mL
1 tsp.	salt	5 mL
1 cup	whipping cream, or more	250 mL
3 tbsp.	melted butter	45 mL

Preheat oven to 400°F (200°C). Sift first 4 ingredients into a bowl. Add whipping cream. I always have to add a little milk, about ¼ cup (60 mL), to make a soft dough. It depends on the flour. Turn dough onto a floured board and pat to ¾" (2 cm) thickness. Cut with a sharp cutter. Dip biscuits in melted butter, place on an ungreased cookie sheet and bake for 20 - 25 minutes, until light golden brown. You be the judge. **Makes 12 biscuits.**

NOTE: If your cutter is not sharp you will seal the edges of the biscuits and they won't rise as high.

POTATO SCONES

These are wonderful with jam or cheese.

1 cup	all-purpose flour	250 mL
4 tsp.	baking powder	20 mL
1 tsp.	salt	5 mL
1 tsp.	sugar	5 mL
2 tbsp.	butter or margarine	30 mL
¾ cup	mashed potato	175 mL
½ cup	milk, or more	125 mL

Preheat oven to 375°F (190°C). Sift together first 4 ingredients. Cut butter and potato into flour mixture. Stir in milk and knead lightly on a floured surface. Pat dough into a round shape, ½" (1.3 cm) thickness. Cut into 8 wedges and place on a greased cookie sheet. Bake for 20-25 minutes. Serve warm with honey, jam or jelly. **Makes 8 scones.**

BRUNCH

Golden Cheese Wheel, page 14
Red & Green Pepper Salad, page 63
Sour Cream Coffee Cake, page 25
Date Oat Squares, page 183
Three-Layer Date Squares, page 182
Cherry Slice, page 182
Lemon Cream Cheese Bars, page 180

SCONES — MAKE YOUR OWN MIX

SCONE MIX:

10 cups	all-purpose flour	2.5 L
⅓ cup	baking powder	75 mL
1 tbsp.	salt	15 mL
1 lb.	shortening or margarine	500 g

Combine flour, baking powder and salt; work the shortening into the flour with a pastry blender. Store in a covered container. Refrigerate.

TO MAKE SCONES:

1	egg, beaten	1
½ cup	buttermilk or milk	125 mL
⅓ cup	sugar	75 mL
½ cup	currants or raisins	125 mL
2½ cups	scone mix	625 mL
1	egg yolk	1
1 tbsp.	sugar	15 mL

Preheat oven to 400°F (200°C). Beat the egg and milk together, stir in sugar. Add currants or raisins. Stir in liquid ingredients. Divide dough in 2, shape into circles of about ½" (1.3 cm) thickness. Cut like a pie into 4-6 pieces. Brush top of scones with 1 egg yolk beaten with a tbsp. (15 mL) of sugar. You can sprinkle tops with sugar if you wish. Bake for 20 minutes, or until golden. **Makes 8-12 scones.**

VARIATION: Sprinkle with cinnamon before baking.

NOTE: When you use currants, always wash them with hot water. Be sure the grit is removed.

BAKING HINTS:

- After you shape the loaves and before the dough starts to rise, brush loaves of bread dough with melted butter to prevent the dough from drying out.

- Grease only the bottom of muffin tins. Muffins will then be nicely shaped; there will be no rim around the top edge.

- For a crusty loaf of bread, put a pan of water in the oven. The steam makes the crust crisp. Also brush bread with cold water every 20 minutes as it bakes.

- To test if bread is done, remove loaf from pan and tap on bottom. It will sound hollow if done.

SUNSHINE MUFFINS

2 cups	whole-wheat flour	500 mL
1 cup	brown or white sugar	250 mL
2 tsp.	baking soda	10 mL
1 tbsp.	cinnamon	15 mL
2 cups	grated carrots	500 mL
1/3 cup	chopped, dried apricots	75 mL
1/3 cup	sunflower seeds	75 mL
1/3 cup	chocolate chips	75 mL
1/3 cup	coconut	75 mL
1	banana, mashed	1
3	eggs	3
1 cup	vegetable oil	250 mL
2 tsp.	vanilla	10 mL

Combine flour, sugar, baking soda and cinnamon and mix well. Stir in carrots, apricots, sunflower seeds, chocolate chips, coconut and banana. Beat together eggs, oil and vanilla. Stir into flour mixture until just moistened. Spoon into greased muffin cups and bake at 350°F (180°C) for 20 minutes. **Makes 2 dozen medium muffins.**

VARIATION: Vary ingredients to suit taste. Try substituting poppy seeds for sunflower seeds and grated apples for carrots.

WHOLE-WHEAT LOAF

2 cups	whole-wheat flour	500 mL
2 cups	all-purpose flour	500 mL
2 tsp.	baking powder	10 mL
1 tsp.	baking soda	5 mL
1 tsp.	salt	5 mL
2	eggs, well-beaten	2
2 cups	buttermilk	500 mL
3 tbsp.	brown sugar or 1/2 cup (125 mL) fancy molasses	45 mL
1/2 cup	rolled oats or poppy seeds	125 mL

Combine dry ingredients. In a bowl, beat eggs, add buttermilk and sugar or molasses. Mix dry ingredients into the egg mixture and knead. Add a bit more flour if dough is sticky. Grease a cookie sheet. Divide dough in 2 and make 2 round loaves. Roll loaves in rolled oats or sprinkle with poppy seeds. Cut a cross on each loaf. Bake at 375°F (190°C) for 45-50 minutes. Serve hot with baked beans and salad. **Makes 2 loaves.**

CARROT BRAN MUFFINS

1¼ cups	whole-wheat or all-purpose flour	300 mL
1¼ cups	bran cereal flakes	300 mL
1 tsp.	baking powder	5 mL
1 tsp.	baking soda	5 mL
½ tsp.	salt	2 mL
½ tsp.	nutmeg	2 mL
1 tsp.	cinnamon	5 mL
2	eggs	2
¾ cup	grated carrots	175 mL
½ cup	packed brown sugar	125 mL
½ cup	vegetable oil	125 mL
1 cup	buttermilk or sour milk	250 mL
½ cup	raisins	125 mL

In large bowl, combine flour, cereal, baking powder, baking soda, salt and spices. In a separate bowl, beat eggs. Stir in carrots, brown sugar, oil and buttermilk. Add to dry ingredients, stirring just until moistened. Stir in raisins. Spoon into well-greased muffin tins or paper baking cups. Bake at 400°F (200°C) for 20 or 25 minutes, or until tops spring back when touched. **Makes 12 medium muffins.**

ORANGE BRAN MUFFINS

2	eggs	2
½ cup	vegetable oil	125 mL
1 cup	brown sugar	250 mL
1 cup	milk	250 mL
2 cups	whole-wheat flour	500 mL
1½ cups	bran	375 mL
1 tsp.	baking soda	5 mL
2 tsp.	baking powder	10 mL
1 tsp.	salt	5 mL
1 cup	sunflower seeds	250 mL
1	orange, unpeeled, put through food chopper	1

Beat together eggs, oil, sugar, add milk. Add dry ingredients and ground orange. Fill greased muffin tins ⅔ full. Bake for 30-40 minutes at 350°F (180°C). **Makes 12 large muffins.**

APPLE MUFFINS

2	eggs	2
2/3 cup	vegetable oil	150 mL
1/2 cup	brown sugar	125 mL
1/2 cup-2 tbsp.	white sugar (or all brown sugar)	95 mL
1 tsp.	vanilla	5 mL
2 1/2 cups	all-purpose flour	625 mL
1 tbsp.	baking powder	15 mL
1 tsp.	salt	5 mL
1 cup	milk or apple juice	250 mL
1/2 cup	chopped nuts	125 mL
2	apples, grated	2
2 tbsp.	sugar	30 mL
1 tsp.	cinnamon	5 mL

In a large bowl, beat eggs, oil, sugars and vanilla. Stir in flour, baking powder and salt. Add milk or apple juice. Add nuts and apples. Fill greased muffin tins 2/3 full. Mix together 2 tbsp. (30 mL) sugar and cinnamon and sprinkle on top of muffins. Bake at 375°F (190°C) for 25-30 minutes. **Makes 12 large muffins.**

VARIATIONS: Omit nuts if desired and substitute 1 cup (250 mL) fresh or frozen blueberries, raspberries or chopped peaches, apricots, etc. for the apples.

RHUBARB MUFFINS

1	egg	1
1 1/2 cups	brown sugar	375 mL
2/3 cup	vegetable oil	150 mL
1 tsp.	vanilla	5 mL
2 cups	finely chopped rhubarb	500 mL
2 1/2 cups	all-purpose flour	625 mL
1 tsp.	baking soda	5 mL
1 1/2 tsp.	baking powder	7 mL
1/2 tsp.	salt	2 mL
1 cup	sour milk or buttermilk	250 mL
1/3 cup	white sugar	75 mL
1 tsp.	cinnamon	5 mL

In a large bowl, beat egg, sugar, oil and vanilla until light. Add the rhubarb. Stir in dry ingredients until just mixed together. Stir in milk. Fill well-greased muffin tins 3/4 full. Combine 1/3 cup (75 mL) sugar and cinnamon and sprinkle over muffins. Bake at 350°F (180°C) for 25-30 minutes. **Makes 18 large muffins.**

OATMEAL MUFFIN MIX

4 cups	rolled oats	1 L
2 cups	all-purpose flour	500 mL
2½ cups	brown sugar	625 mL
4 tsp.	baking powder	20 mL
1 tbsp.	salt	15 mL
1½ cups	butter or margarine	375 mL
1 cup	raisins	250 mL
1 cup	nuts	250 mL

Mix all ingredients together; cover and store in the refrigerator.

Oatmeal Muffins

3 cups	Oatmeal Muffin Mix	750 mL
1	egg, beaten	1
½ cup	milk	125 mL
½ cup	fresh or frozen blueberries (optional)	125 mL

Combine all ingredients and fill greased muffin tins. Bake at 350°F (180°C) for 25 minutes. **Makes 12 large muffins.**

CORN BREAD

My father loved this recipe. It is often called Johnny Cake.

1 cup	all-purpose flour	250 mL
1 cup	yellow cornmeal	250 mL
½ cup	sugar	125 mL
1 tsp.	salt	5 mL
4 tsp.	baking powder	20 mL
2	eggs	2
1 cup	milk	250 mL
½ cup	vegetable oil	125 mL

Mix together flour, cornmeal, sugar, salt and baking powder. Combine eggs, milk and oil. Add to dry ingredients. Mix just until well-blended. Do not over mix. Pour batter into a 9" (23 cm) square greased pan. Bake at 350°F (180°C) for 25 minutes. **Makes 12 muffins.**

VARIATION: For Cornmeal Muffins, pour batter into greased muffin tins and bake for 20-25 minutes.

See photograph on page 69.

APPLE OR PLUM COFFEE CAKE

This is a variation of a cake my mother made. When her family was in Ukraine, they grew their own plums and apples and this was a family favorite.

5-6	apples or 8 plums	5-6
½ cup	butter or margarine	125 mL
¾ cup	sugar	175 mL
1	egg	1
1 tsp.	vanilla	5 mL
1¼ cups	flour	300 mL
2 tsp.	baking powder	10 mL
½ tsp.	salt	2 mL
½ cup	milk	125 mL

TOPPING:

¾ cup	brown sugar	175 mL
3 tbsp.	flour	45 mL
1 tsp.	cinnamon	5 mL
½ cup	chopped nuts (optional)	125 mL

Pare apples and slice thickly or cut plums in half and discard the pits. Cream together butter, sugar, egg and vanilla. Sift together flour, baking powder and salt. Add dry ingredients alternately with milk to creamed mixture. Spread dough in greased 9" (23 cm) square pan. Top with rows of apples or plums. Combine topping ingredients and sprinkle evenly over the fruit. Bake at 350°F (180°C) for 40 minutes. Cut into squares and serve hot with whipped cream or plain. **Serves 10 to 12.**

VARIATION: For Blueberry Coffee Cake, use 1½ cups (375 mL) fresh or frozen blueberries instead of apples or plums. For Peach Kuchen, substitute peaches for apples and pour a mixture of 1 egg yolk and ¼ cup (60 mL) whipping cream over the hot cake, in the pan.

BAKING HINTS:

- Always have the flour at room temperature; this will help the bread to rise.

- Keep your walnuts or pecans in an airtight container in the freezer. I always shell my own walnuts and freeze them.

- Nut breads should be cut when the loaves are completely cold. Cut with a sharp knife.

- After your bread is baked, always remove the bread from the pan and set on a wire rack to cool.

SOUR CREAM COFFEE CAKE

2 cups	all-purpose flour	500 mL
1 tsp.	baking powder	5 mL
1 tsp.	baking soda	5 mL
½ tsp.	salt	2 mL
1 cup	sugar	250 mL
½ cup	butter	125 mL
2	eggs	2
1 tsp.	vanilla	5 mL
1 cup	sour cream	250 mL
½ cup	sugar	125 mL
½ cup	chopped walnuts or pecans (optional)	125 mL
1 tsp.	cinnamon	5 mL

Mix together flour, baking powder, soda and salt. Cream sugar, butter, eggs and vanilla thoroughly. Add dry ingredients alternately with sour cream to creamed mixture. Mix until smooth. Butter and flour a 9" (23 cm) square pan or tube pan. Combine ½ cup (125 mL) sugar, nuts and cinnamon. Spread half the batter in the pan. Sprinkle with half the sugar mixture. Add the rest of the batter and top with remaining topping. Bake at 350°F (180°C) for 45-60 minutes. **Serves 12.**

See photograph on page 17.

BANANA BREAD

I've used this recipe for many years. My grandson, Stephen, loves it.

2	eggs	2
½ cup	vegetable oil	125 mL
1½ cups	sugar	375 mL
½ tsp.	salt	2 mL
1 tsp.	vanilla	5 mL
⅓ cup	sour milk or buttermilk	75 mL
2	ripe bananas	2
1¾ cups	all-purpose flour	425 mL
1 tsp.	baking soda	5 mL
1 cup	chopped walnuts or pecans	250 mL

Preheat oven to 350°F (180°C). Grease and flour a 5 x 9" (13 x 23 cm) loaf pan. Cream eggs, oil, sugar, salt, vanilla, milk and mashed bananas. Add flour, soda and nuts. Mix gently and pour into prepared loaf pan. Bake about 1 hour. When done, loaf is light brown and cracks a bit on the top. Test with a toothpick in the middle of the cake. **Makes 1 loaf.**

LEMON LOAF

This loaf has a lovely tart yet sweet flavor.

1 cup	sugar	250 mL
½ cup	butter or margarine	125 mL
1 tbsp.	grated lemon rind	15 mL
2	eggs	2
1½ cups	all-purpose flour	375 mL
½ tsp.	salt	2 mL
1 tsp.	baking powder	5 mL
½ cup	milk	125 mL
½ cup	chopped nuts (optional)	125 mL
¼ cup	sugar	60 mL
1	lemon, juice of	1

In a bowl, cream the sugar and butter. Add lemon rind and eggs. Sift flour, salt, baking powder and add to creamed mixture alternately with milk. Stir in nuts. Pour into greased and floured 5 x 9" (13 x 23 cm) loaf pan or 2 smaller ones. Bake at 350°F (180°C) for 35-40 minutes for the large loaf, 25-30 minutes for the smaller loaves. Test with a toothpick. If it comes out clean, the cake is done. Boil together ¼ cup (60 mL) sugar and lemon juice and pour over loaf after it is out of the oven. Let loaf cool in pan. **Makes 1 large or 2 small loaves.**

BLUEBERRY ORANGE LOAF

½ tsp.	baking soda	2 mL
2 tsp.	baking powder	10 mL
2 cups	all-purpose flour	500 mL
¾ cup	sugar	175 mL
¾ tsp.	salt	3 mL
1 tbsp.	grated orange rind	15 mL
¼ cup	orange juice	60 mL
¼ cup	melted butter	60 mL
¾ cup	milk	175 mL
1	egg, beaten	1
1½ cups	frozen blueberries	375 mL
½ cup	chopped nuts	125 mL

Sift dry ingredients into a bowl. Combine orange rind, orange juice, melted butter, milk and egg and stir in flour mixture. Mix well. Spread ⅓ of batter into a greased 5 x 9" (13 x 23 cm) loaf pan, sprinkle with half of berries and nuts. Cover with ⅓ of batter and remaining fruit and nuts. Top with remaining batter. Bake at 350°F (180°C) for 50 minutes. **Makes 1 loaf.**

ZUCCHINI LOAF

2 cups	all-purpose flour	500 mL
1½ cups	brown sugar	375 mL
2 tsp.	baking powder	10 mL
1 tsp.	baking soda	5 mL
1 tbsp.	cinnamon	15 mL
1 tsp.	salt	5 mL
1 cup	oil	250 mL
1 tsp.	vanilla	5 mL
2	eggs	2
2 cups	grated zucchini	500 mL
½ cup	raisins	125 mL
1 cup	chopped walnuts or pecans	250 mL

In a large bowl, combine flour, sugar, baking powder, baking soda, cinnamon, salt, oil, vanilla and eggs. Beat at medium speed until light. Stir in zucchini, raisins and half of nuts. Mix well. Pour into 3 greased and floured 4 x 8" (10 x 20 cm) loaf pans or a 9 x 13" (23 x 33 cm) pan. Sprinkle remaining nuts on top. Bake at 350°F (180°C) for 40-50 minutes for 9 x 13" (23 x 33 cm) pan or 30-40 minutes for loaf pans. **Serves 14.**

DATE AND NUT BREAD

This is an old, old recipe. I have used it for over 50 years.

1 cup	boiling water	250 mL
2 cups	chopped dates	500 mL
1 cup	chopped walnuts	250 mL
½ cup	shortening, butter or margarine	125 mL
1 cup	brown sugar	250 mL
2	eggs	2
2 cups	cake or all-purpose flour	500 mL
1 tsp.	salt	5 mL
1 tsp.	baking soda	5 mL
⅓ cup	water	75 mL

In a large bowl, pour boiling water over chopped dates and nuts and let stand. Cream shortening and sugar, add eggs and beat until light. Add flour and salt to creamed mixture. Add soda to date mixture and combine with creamed mixture. Add ⅓ cup (75 mL) water. Pour into 2, 5 x 9" (13 x 23 cm) or 3, 4 x 8" (10 x 20 cm) loaf pans that have been well-greased and floured. Bake at 350°F (180°C) for 45-50 minutes for large loaf pans and 30-40 minutes for smaller pans. Test with a toothpick. If toothpick comes out clean, it's done. **Makes 2 large or 3 small loaves.**

PLAIN DOUGHNUTS

Homemade doughnuts are always a childhood favorite, a special treat.

3 tbsp.	butter	45 mL
1 cup	sugar	250 mL
3	eggs	3
4 cups	all-purpose flour	1 L
4 tsp.	baking powder	20 mL
1/2 tsp.	nutmeg	2 mL
1 tsp.	salt	5 mL
1 cup	milk	250 mL

Cream butter, sugar and eggs, beating until very light. Sift together flour, baking powder, nutmeg and salt and add alternately with milk to creamed mixture. Roll dough 1/4" (1 cm) thick and cut with doughnut cutter. Deep-fry at 375°F (190°C). The doughnuts should rise to the top almost immediately. When brown on one side, turn and brown other side. Roll doughnuts in granulated sugar. Put on paper towels to cool. They freeze very well. **Makes about 4 dozen doughnuts.**

THE BEST RAISED DOUGHNUTS

My cousin Pauline makes these light lovely doughnuts and sells them at the farmer's market in Bonneville.

1 tbsp.	yeast (1 env.)	15 mL
1 tsp.	sugar	5 mL
3/4 cup	warm water	175 mL
3	large eggs, well-beaten	3
1/2 cup	sugar	125 mL
1/2 cup	vegetable oil	125 mL
2 cups	warm water	500 mL
1 tsp.	salt	5 mL
7 1/2-8 cups	flour	1.8-2 L
1 tbsp.	butter	15 mL

Soak yeast and 1 tsp. (5 mL) of sugar for 8-10 minutes in 3/4 cup (175 mL) water. In a large bowl, beat eggs until light, about 5 minutes. Add yeast, sugar, oil, water and salt. Add enough flour to make a very soft dough, adding a little bit at a time, until dough is not sticky. Butter dough, cover and let rise, about 1 hour, until double. Punch the dough down and let rise again. Roll out to about 1/2" (1.3 cm) thickness and cut with doughnut cutter. Place doughnuts on tea towel and let rise for an hour or so. Deep-fry at 375°F (190°C). Drain on paper towels. Roll doughnuts in granulated sugar if you like. **Makes about 3 1/2 dozen doughnuts.**

NOTE: These doughnuts freeze very well.

CINNAMON BUNS

This sweet dough makes light fluffy cinnamon buns or you can make it into buns and bake as dinner buns, page 30.

1 tbsp.	sugar	15 mL
½ cup	warm water	125 mL
1 tbsp.	yeast (1 env.)	15 mL
½ cup	milk	125 mL
4 tbsp.	butter or margarine	60 mL
¼ cup	sugar	60 mL
1 tsp.	salt	5 mL
½ cup	cold water	125 mL
2	eggs, well-beaten	2
4-5 cups	all-purpose flour	1-1.25 L
½ cup	butter or margarine at room temperature	125 mL
1 cup	brown sugar	250 mL
1 tbsp.	cinnamon, or more if you prefer	15 mL
½ cup	raisins, washed and dried (optional)	125 mL

Dissolve sugar in warm water and sprinkle yeast over, let stand for 10 minutes. Scald milk, add butter, sugar, salt, cold water and eggs and mix. Combine milk and yeast mixtures. Beat in the flour. When dough is thick, knead for about 5 minutes. This makes a soft dough. Add more flour if needed. Grease top of dough, cover and let rise until doubled in bulk, about 1 hour. Roll out dough into 12 x 20" (30 x 50 cm) rectangle and spread with butter or margarine. Combine remaining ingredients and spread evenly over dough. Roll dough as a jelly roll. With a sharp knife, cut into 1½" (4 cm) slices. Place rolls in a 9 x 13" (23 x 33 cm) greased pan, leaving room for them to rise. If you like a caramel bottom, sprinkle pan bottom with ½ cup (125 mL) brown sugar. Let rise about 40 minutes. Bake at 350°F (180°C) for 25-30 minutes. Turn out on a cake rack as soon as you take them out of the oven. **Makes 24 cinnamon buns.**

PIZZA DOUGH

1 cup	warm water	250 mL
1 tsp.	sugar	5 mL
1 tbsp.	yeast (1 env.)	15 mL
2½ cups	all-purpose flour, or more	625 mL
3 tbsp.	vegetable oil	45 mL
1 tsp.	salt	5 mL

In a bowl, combine water, sugar and yeast and let stand for 5 minutes. Add remaining ingredients and knead dough. Let dough rest for 10 minutes. Press into a pizza pan. Top with your favorite tomato sauce, cheese, sliced vegetables and/or meat. Bake on an ungreased cookie sheet at 400°F (200°C) for 20-25 minutes. **This makes enough dough for a 14"(35 cm) pizza or 2 small pizzas.**

DINNER BUNS

1 tbsp.	yeast (1 env.)	15 mL
2 cups	very warm water	500 mL
¼ cup	sugar	60 mL
2	large or 3 small eggs, well-beaten	2
¼ cup	oil	60 mL
	salt	
5 cups	all-purpose flour, approximately	1.25 L

Dissolve yeast in the water and sugar. Let soak for about 8 minutes. In a large bowl, mix together yeast mixture, eggs, oil and salt. Stir in the flour and knead for 5-8 minutes. The dough should be soft but not sticky. Grease top of dough, cover and let rise for about 2 hours. Punch down dough. Shape dough into buns or make 1 pan of buns and a loaf of bread. Place buns in greased 9 x 13" (23 x 33 cm) pans or use cookie sheets with a rim. Let rise for about 1-1½ hours. Bake at 350°F (180°C) for about 30 minutes. Remove bread or buns from the pans as soon as you take them from the oven. Put them on a rack to cool. **Makes 24 buns.**

BATTER ROLLS

These quick breakfast or dinner rolls are very light. They are easy to make; you don't have to worry about dough consistency. It is sticky, like a thick batter.

1 cup	milk	250 mL
2 tbsp.	sugar	30 mL
½ cup	shortening, butter or margarine	125 mL
2 tbsp.	yeast (2 env.)	30 mL
1 cup	warm water	250 mL
1 tbsp.	sugar	15 mL
3 cups	all-purpose flour	750 mL

Scald milk, add 2 tbsp. (30 mL) sugar and shortening. Stir to dissolve shortening. Cool to warm. Let yeast dissolve in water and 1 tbsp. (15 mL) sugar for 10 minutes. Add yeast to lukewarm milk. Add flour to liquid mixture and stir to mix thoroughly. Cover and let rise, away from drafts, for about 1 hour. Stir the mixture down and let it stand for 10 minutes. Grease muffin tins and fill them ¾ full of dough. Let rise about ½ hour, bake at 375°F (190°C) for 20-30 minutes. Serve hot. **Makes 12 rolls.**

WHITE BREAD

Don't be afraid to try bread baking, even if you don't have loaf pans. Use 1¹/₂ lb. (750 g) coffee tins or a casserole. My mother would even put shaped loaves on greased cabbage leaves because she didn't have enough bread pans. The loaves were very crusty and the undersides showed the imprint of the veined cabbage leaves.

1 tsp.	sugar	5 mL
¹/₂ cup	very warm water	125 mL
2 tbsp.	yeast (2 env.)	30 mL
4 cups	very warm water	1 L
4 tbsp.	butter, margarine or lard	60 mL
2 tbsp.	sugar	30 mL
1 tbsp.	salt	15 mL
7 cups	all-purpose flour, or more	1.75 L

In a small bowl, dissolve first sugar in water. Sprinkle yeast over. Let stand for about 10 minutes. In a large bowl, combine warm water, butter, 2 tbsp. (30 mL) sugar and salt. The other ingredients will cool the water a bit. Add yeast mixture and flour. Knead the dough for about 10 minutes, first in the bowl, then turn onto a floured counter and knead until smooth. Butter the dough and let rise in a warm place for 1 hour or more. Knead down and let rise again. Grease 4 or 5, 5 x 9" (13 x 23 cm) loaf pans. Cut dough and shape loaves. Place dough in pans; pans should be about half full; let rise until doubled in bulk, about 1 hour. Bake for 40-50 minutes at 350°F (180°C). Remove from pans immediately; put on racks to cool. **Makes 4-5 loaves.**

FRENCH BREAD

2 cups	warm water	500 mL
1 tbsp.	yeast (1 env.)	15 mL
1 tbsp.	salt	15 mL
6-6¹/₂ cups	all-purpose flour	1.5-1.6 L
	cornmeal	

Put water in large bowl. Sprinkle yeast over and let stand until dissolved. Beat in salt and 3 cups (750 mL) of flour. Mix thoroughly. Add the rest of the flour and knead for 5 minutes or more. Place dough in bowl, cover and allow to rise until doubled in size, about 1 hour. Cut dough into 3-4 equal pieces. Roll each piece to about 12-14" (30-35 cm). Place loaves on cookie sheets sprinkled with cornmeal. Slash each loaf diagonally with a sharp knife in 2-3 places. Let dough rise, uncovered, until doubled in size, about 1 hour. Bake at 375°F (190°C) for 30-40 minutes. Put a pan of water in the oven; the steam will make a crusty bread. As the bread bakes, brush it with cold water every 20 minutes. Do not grease the loaves. **Makes 3-4 loaves.**

See photograph on page 123.

MONKEY BREAD

A tender, light pull-apart loaf.

1 tbsp.	yeast (1 env.)	15 mL
1 tbsp.	sugar	15 mL
½ cup	warm water	125 mL
2 cups	milk, scalded and cooled	500 mL
1 cup	butter, divided	250 mL
1 tsp.	salt	5 mL
3	eggs at room temperature, well-beaten	3
6 cups	all-purpose flour	1.5 L

Dissolve the yeast and sugar in warm water for 8 minutes. Add milk, ¼ cup (60 mL) butter, salt and eggs. Beat in half the flour. Stir in remaining flour. Let dough rise, about 1 hour. Roll out dough to 1" (2.5 cm) thickness and cut with a 2" (5 cm) cookie cutter or use a juice glass dipped in flour. Dip rounds in remaining butter, melted, and put in an angel food tin with a solid bottom. Let rise until doubled in bulk and bake at 350°F (180°C) for 30 minutes. Remove bread from pan. Serve warm. Just pull apart. **This will make 2 pans of monkey bread.**

WHOLE-WHEAT BREAD

1 tbsp.	sugar	15 mL
2 cups	water (very warm but not hot)	500 mL
2 tbsp.	yeast (2 env.)	30 mL
1 tsp.	salt	5 mL
2 tbsp.	fancy molasses	30 mL
2 cups	all-purpose flour	500 mL
3 cups	whole-wheat flour, or more	750 mL

In a large bowl, dissolve sugar in water and sprinkle yeast over. Let stand 5-8 minutes. Add remaining ingredients to yeast mixture. Add more or less flour as required, the dough should be smooth and not sticky. When dough is mixed, lightly flour the counter and knead the dough about 5-6 minutes, until smooth. Lightly butter dough; let rise for 1 hour or until doubled in bulk. Knead dough again and let rise for about 1/2 hour. Make into 2 loaves or you can braid a loaf. To make braid, take half the dough, cut it in half and roll each piece until about 10" (25 cm) long and braid. Place in a greased 4 x 9" (10 x 23 cm) pan. Put the other half of the dough, in a buttered coffee can or another loaf pan. Use your imagination as to the use of pans. Bake at 350°F (180°C) for 30-40 minutes. **Makes 2 loaves.**

See photograph on page 51.

CHEDDAR CHEESE BREAD

1 tbsp.	yeast (1 env.)	15 mL
½ cup	warm water	125 mL
2 tsp.	sugar	10 mL
3 cups	all-purpose flour	750 mL
1 cup	whole-wheat flour	250 mL
1 tsp.	salt	5 mL
1¼ cups	grated Cheddar cheese, divided	300 mL
2 cups	milk	500 mL

Soak yeast in water and sugar. Let stand 5 minutes. Measure flours, salt and 1 cup (250 mL) cheese into a large bowl. Scald milk and cool to lukewarm. Mix milk with yeast. Add to flour mixture and knead for 10 minutes. Let rise in a warm place, not longer than 30 minutes. Divide dough into 3 pieces. Roll each piece into a 16" (41 cm) long roll; braid the 3 pieces. Grease a cookie sheet and put braid to rise until doubled in bulk, about 1½ hours. Grease braided bread and sprinkle with remaining cheese. Bake at 350°F (180°C) for 40-50 minutes. Serve warm with baked beans and a salad or coleslaw. **Makes 1 braided loaf.**

BRAN & WHOLE-WHEAT BREAD

1 cup	warm water	250 mL
1 tsp.	sugar	5 mL
1 tbsp.	yeast (1 env.)	15 mL
1 cup	milk, scalded	250 mL
1 tbsp.	butter or margarine	15 mL
2 tbsp.	fancy molasses	30 mL
1 cup	bran	250 mL
4 cups	whole-wheat flour	1 L

Combine water, sugar and yeast. Let stand for 10 minutes. Add remaining ingredients to yeast mixture. Knead for 5 minutes. Set to rise. When doubled in bulk, about 1 hour, make into 2 loaves and place in 2 greased 4 x 9" (10 x 23 cm) loaf pans. Let rise again until doubled, about 1 hour. Bake at 350°F (180°C) for 40 minutes. Remove bread from pans as soon as you remove the bread from the oven. **Makes 2 loaves.**

NOTE: Grease only the bottoms of loaf pans. The ungreased sides provide a surface for the batter to cling to while rising during baking, which will help to form a rounded top.

CRUSTY BROWN BREAD WITH SEEDS

Use your imagination — try baking bread in unusual pots and shapes.

2 cups	whole-wheat flour	500 mL
3 cups	all-purpose flour	750 mL
1 cup	natural wheat bran or All-Bran cereal	250 mL
1/2 cup	flax seeds	125 mL
1/4 cup	sunflower seeds	60 mL
1/4 cup	poppy seeds	60 mL
1 tbsp.	salt	15 mL
2 tbsp.	instant yeast (2 env.)	30 mL
2 cups	hot water, 125°F (50°C)	500 mL
1/2 cup	vegetable oil	125 mL
1/2 cup	fancy molasses	125 mL
1 tbsp.	vinegar	15 mL

Combine flours, cereal and seeds in a large bowl. Add salt and yeast. Heat water; add oil, molasses and vinegar. Mix liquid ingredients into the dry ingredients. Turn out onto a floured counter and knead for at least 10 minutes, adding a bit of flour if dough sticks to counter. Let dough rest for 10-15 minutes. Shape into 2 loaves. Place in well-greased 5 x 9" (12 x 23 cm) loaf pans and let rise until doubled in bulk, about 1 hour. Bake at 350°F (180°C) for 40 minutes. Put a pan of water in the oven to make bread crusty. Cool on rack. **Makes 2 loaves.**

VARIATION: Try baking this bread in 7" (18 cm) clay flower pots. Scrub pots well; dry and oil with vegetable oil. Put them in a cold oven and heat to 300°F (150°C) for 30 minutes. Turn off oven and leave pots in oven until cool. Repeat oiling and heating process 4 times before baking bread in pots. Cover hole in pot with a piece of foil.

See photograph on page 51.

EASTER BABKA

1/2 cup	warm water	125 mL
1 tsp.	sugar	5 mL
3 tbsp.	yeast (3 env.)	45 mL
2 cups	milk, scalded	500 mL
6	egg yolks	6
2	whole eggs	2
1 cup	sugar	250 mL
1/2 lb.	butter or margarine, melted	250 g
1 tbsp.	salt	15 mL
1 tsp.	vanilla	5 mL
8-10 cups	all-purpose flour	2-2.5 L
1 cup	golden raisins, well-washed	250 mL
1	lemon, grated rind of	1

EASTER BABKA

Continued

In a small bowl, combine warm water, 1 tsp. (5 mL) sugar and yeast and let stand for 5-8 minutes. Cool scalded milk. Beat egg yolks and eggs 5-8 minutes, until very light. Combine with milk, 1 cup (250 mL) sugar, melted butter, salt and vanilla. Add yeast and mix in flour. Add raisins and lemon rind. This should be a soft dough. Let rise in a warm place, about 1 hour. Punch down and let rise again for another hour. Shape dough into loaves or use well-greased 1½ or 2 lb. (750 g-1 kg) coffee cans. Fill cans half full and let dough rise. Bake at 325°F (160°C) for 40-50 minutes. When you take the loaves out of oven, remove from cans and put them on a soft towel; turn while cooling. **Makes about 5 loaves.**

NOTE: Freeze as soon as cool if you are not planning to use immediately. The eggs cause this bread to dry out quickly.

HOT CROSS BUNS WITH POTATOES

1 tbsp.	sugar	15 mL
1 cup	warm water	250 mL
2 tbsp.	yeast (2 env.)	30 mL
6 cups	all-purpose flour, or more if needed	1.5 L
½ cup	sugar	125 mL
1 tbsp.	salt	15 mL
1 tsp.	cinnamon	5 mL
½ tsp.	nutmeg	2 mL
¼ tsp.	allspice	1 mL
½ cup	milk	125 mL
½ cup	butter or margarine	125 mL
3	eggs, beaten	3
1 cup	mashed potatoes	250 mL
1 cup	diced mixed peel	250 mL
1 cup	raisins, washed and dried	250 mL
	icing sugar	
	milk	

Dissolve 1 tbsp. (15 mL) sugar in water, sprinkle with yeast and let stand for about 8 minutes. In a large bowl, combine flour, sugar, salt and spices. Scald milk, add butter to melt; cool mixture to lukewarm. Add beaten eggs. Stir into flour mixture. Add yeast mixture and potatoes. Knead all together. Add peel and raisins and knead until mixed. The dough should be soft. Grease dough and let rise in a warm place, about 1 hour. Shape dough into buns and place on greased baking sheets with rims. Let rise for about 1 hour; bake at 375°F (190°C) for 25-30 minutes. When cold, make the form of a cross on each bun with icing made with icing sugar mixed with a bit of milk. **Makes about 2 dozen buns.**

HOLIDAY BREAD

This makes an attractive and delicious Christmas gift.

1 tsp.	sugar	5 mL
½ cup	water	125 mL
1 tbsp.	yeast (1 env.)	15 mL
1 cup	milk	250 mL
3 tbsp.	butter or margarine	45 mL
2	eggs, well-beaten	2
1 tsp.	salt	5 mL
½ cup	sugar	125 mL
3 cups	all-purpose flour, or more	750 mL
1 cup	golden raisins, washed and dried	250 mL
½ cup	chopped apricots	125 mL
½ cup	toasted, chopped almonds	125 mL
2 tbsp.	grated orange peel	30 mL
1	egg white	1
1 tbsp.	water	15 mL

Dissolve 1 tsp. (5 mL) sugar in ½ cup (125 mL) water, sprinkle with yeast and let stand for 5 minutes. Scald milk; add butter; cool. When milk is cool, add beaten eggs, salt, sugar and yeast mixture. Stir liquid ingredients into flour. Add fruit, nuts, orange peel, knead for 5-8 minutes. Butter dough and put in bowl to rise for 1-1½ hours. Knead down and cut dough in half. Cut each half in 3 pieces and roll out about 14" (36 cm) long. Braid dough and place loaves on greased cookie sheets. You could also use coffee cans or loaf pans for different shapes. Let rise in warm place until nearly doubled in bulk, about 1 hour. Brush with egg white beaten with 1 tbsp. (15 ml) of water. Bake at 350°F (180°C) for 30 minutes or more. When cool, decorate with icing and halved red and green cherries. **Makes 2 braided loaves.**

See photograph on the back cover.

HELPFUL HINT:

• When using milk in bread, doughnuts or buns, always scald it. Heat milk in a pot, watching carefully so it doesn't boil. Just before the milk boils, remove from heat and cool.

COUNTRY
F L A V O R S

Appetizers
&
Drinks

FRUIT DIP

This is an absolutely wonderful dip or sauce for fresh fruit.

5	egg yolks	5
1/2 cup	white sugar	125 mL
1 cup	whipping cream	250 mL
2 tbsp.	Grand Marnier, amaretto or orange juice	30 mL

Beat together egg yolks, sugar and 1/2 cup (125 mL) cream. Put in double boiler and beat while cooking, until thick. Remove from heat and add Grand Marnier, amaretto or orange juice. Put custard in a bowl and cover with plastic wrap until cold. In a cold, small bowl, whip remaining cream until stiff. Fold whipped cream into cold custard. Serve as dip with fresh pineapple, melon, strawberries, apples, pears, peaches or bananas. Or serve over a fruit salad. **Makes 1 1/2 cups (375 mL).**

GUACAMOLE

Make this smooth and rich or make it chunky and spice it up with hot pepper sauce.

2	avocados, pitted and peeled	2
1 tbsp.	grated lemon rind	15 mL
1 tbsp.	lemon juice	15 mL
1	garlic clove, grated	1
1/2 tsp.	salt	2 mL
1/2 cup	mayonnaise	125 mL

In a blender, combine all ingredients until smooth. Place in a bowl, cover and chill. Serve as a dip with fresh vegetables: carrot sticks, cauliflower florets, celery sticks, cucumber slices, broccoli, etc. **Makes about 2 cups (500 mL).**

VARIATION: Chopped, drained fresh tomato adds flavor and color. Also try adding 2 tbsp. (30 mL) finely chopped onion and a drop or 2 of hot pepper sauce.

GREEN CHILI SALSA

I've experimented with many salsa recipes. This one is hot, very good and very easy.

2	large tomatoes, finely chopped	2
1	large onion, finely chopped	1
4	green onions, finely chopped	4
4 tbsp.	finely chopped pickled jalapeño peppers	60 mL
3 tbsp.	vinegar	45 mL
2 tbsp.	jalapeño pickle juice	30 mL

Combine all ingredients, cover and chill until serving time, preferably 4 hours or so. **Makes about 3 cups (750 mL).**

ANTIPASTO

This old favorite can be made ahead and frozen. It is great to have on hand.

2 x 15 oz.	bottles tomato ketchup	2 x 425 mL
15 oz.	bottle hot ketchup	425 mL
1/2 cup	olive oil	125 mL
1	medium head cauliflower, cut into small pieces	1
1	red pepper, finely chopped	1
1	green pepper, finely chopped	1
14 oz.	ripe black olives, chopped	398 mL
1	large carrot, shredded	1
1 cup	chopped olives with pimiento	250 mL
10 oz.	can of mushroom stems and pieces	284 mL
2 x 6.5 oz.	cans solid tuna, broken up	2 x 184 g
2 x 4.5 oz.	cans small shrimp	2 x 128 g
2	garlic cloves, crushed	2
2 cups	chopped sweet pickles	500 mL

In a large pot, combine both the ketchups. Bring to a boil, add remaining ingredients and boil for 10 minutes only. Stir while boiling. When cold, pour into sterilized jars or freeze in plastic containers with tight-fitting lids. Will keep in the refrigerator for 1 week. Serve with tortilla chips or crackers. **Makes 3 quarts (3 L).**

SPICY SEAFOOD DIP

1 cup	mayonnaise	250 mL
1 tbsp.	anchovy paste (optional)	15 mL
½ tsp.	dry mustard	2 mL
½ tsp.	Tabasco sauce	2 mL
1	garlic clove, grated	1
2 tbsp.	vinegar	30 mL
3	eggs, hard-boiled, finely chopped	3
¼ cup	finely chopped olives	60 mL
1 tbsp.	parsley	15 mL
½	medium onion, finely chopped	½

Combine ingredients in order and mix well. Serve with chunks of lobster, shrimp or other seafood. This is also good with nacho chips. **Makes about 2 cups (500 mL).**

SALMON MOLD

2 tbsp.	gelatin (2 env.)	30 mL
½ cup	cold water	125 mL
1 cup	hot chicken broth	250 mL
1 cup	mayonnaise	250 mL
3 tbsp.	chili sauce	45 mL
2 tbsp.	lemon juice	30 ml
2 tbsp.	grated onion	30 mL
½ tsp.	Worcestershire sauce	2 mL
½ tsp.	Ac´cent	2 mL
8 oz.	can salmon	250 g
1 cup	diced celery	250 mL
½ cup	sliced stuffed olives	125 mL

Dissolve gelatin in cold water then add it to the hot chicken broth. Add remaining ingredients, adding salmon, celery and olives last. Pour into mold and chill overnight. You can also add finely chopped green onion. Serve on assorted crackers or dark rye bread. **Serves 10-12.**

CREAM CHEESE PLATTER WITH CRAB

2 x 8 oz.	pkgs. cream cheese	2 x 250 g
1 tbsp.	lemon juice	15 mL
1 tbsp.	Worcestershire sauce	15 mL
1	garlic clove, grated	1
3 tbsp.	mayonnaise	45 mL
8 oz.	bottle seafood sauce	250 mL
4 oz.	can crab meat, or more if you like	115 g
	chives or parsley, chopped	

Cream together cheese, lemon juice, Worcestershire sauce, garlic and mayonnaise until smooth and creamy. Spread the cream cheese on a large round plate. Make a raised border as you spread the cheese mixture. Cover cheese with seafood cocktail sauce. Top it with 1 or 2 cans crab meat. If you use canned crab, squeeze out the water. Sprinkle with fresh chives or parsley. Cover with plastic wrap and put in refrigerator for a few hours or overnight. Serve with different kinds of crackers. **Serves 10-12.**

VARIATIONS: Use shrimp instead of crab meat; try salsa instead of seafood sauce. Top with grated Cheddar, Swiss or mozzarella cheese.

HERBED MUSHROOMS

Serve these quick marinated mushrooms with assorted hor d'oeuvres.

1 lb.	small mushrooms	500 g
½ cup	cider vinegar	125 mL
2 tbsp.	salad oil	30 mL
1	garlic clove, crushed	1
½ tsp.	salt	2 mL
1½ tsp.	sugar	7 mL
4 oz.	jar diced pimientos, drained	398 mL
1 tsp.	dried parsley	5 mL

Brush mushrooms clean. Place in bowl. Mix together the rest of ingredients and pour over mushrooms. Marinate mushrooms for a day or 2. Stir occasionally. Serve with toothpicks. **Serves 4-6.**

DEVILLED EGGS

This old favorite is a must for picnics and summer parties.

6	eggs, hard-boiled	6
3 tbsp.	mayonnaise	45 mL
½ tsp.	mustard	2 mL
¼ tsp.	salt	1 mL
¼ tsp.	pepper	1 mL
	parsley, green onion or paprika to garnish	

Peel eggs. Cut lengthwise into halves. Slip out the yolks. Mash yolks with a fork. Add mayonnaise, mustard, salt and pepper. Mix well. Fill the whites with the egg yolk mixture. Snip parsley or green onion in tiny bits and sprinkle on each egg, or sprinkle with paprika. **Serves 6.**

ROASTED GARLIC HEADS

Choose firm large garlic heads with large cloves. Make a cup for each garlic head with double thickness of foil. Pour a tsp. (5 mL) of olive oil over each head; salt to taste. Pinch foil cup closed. Bake in oven for 30 or 40 minutes at 350°F (180°C). When done, separate cloves and squeeze them out on crackers or fresh French bread. Tasty served with homemade beans.

NOTE: *Be careful not to scorch the garlic, it will get bitter if burned.*

OLIVE AND BLUE CHEESE BALL

8 oz.	cream cheese	250 g
4 oz.	blue cheese	125 g
¼ cup	softened butter or margarine	60 mL
¾ cup	chopped ripe olives	175 mL
¼ cup	chopped green onion	60 mL
¼ tsp.	hot sauce	1 mL
1	garlic clove, minced	1
1/2 cup	chopped pecans, parsley or red and green peppers	125 mL

With an electric mixer, combine all ingredients except pecans. Chill and form into a ball. Roll in nuts, parsley or finely chopped red and green peppers. This can be frozen. Do not freeze cheese balls rolled in peppers. **Serves 10-12.**

CHICKEN LIVER PÂTÉ

Bacon and garlic give this a great flavor. It makes a wonderful gift

1½ lbs.	chicken livers	750 g
¼ lb.	butter (do not substitute)	125 g
2	garlic cloves, finely grated	2
1	large onion, chopped	1
½ lb.	bacon, cut in pieces	250 g
	salt and pepper to taste	

Sauté chicken livers and garlic in all of the butter. Do not brown. Remove livers with slotted spoon. Fry chopped onion in remaining butter until soft but not brown. Add to livers. Wash frying pan and fry bacon until done but not crisp. Chop all ingredients for a coarse texture. Use a meat grinder for a medium texture or a food processor for a fine texture. Mix together with all the butter and bacon fat — you are making a spread. Place in small, deep bowls. To serve, loosen with a knife. Pâté will come out easily. Decorate with cherry tomatoes and serve with crackers or rye bread. May be frozen. **Serves 10-12.**

See photograph on page 123.

SHERRIED CHICKEN LIVER PÂTÉ

Salt pork and thyme are a good combination with the sherry.

¼ lb.	salt pork	125 g
1 lb.	chicken livers	500 g
¼ tsp.	thyme	1 mL
⅛ tsp.	pepper	0.5 mL
1	large onion, chopped	1
1	garlic clove	1
4 tbsp.	sherry	60 mL

Cut salt pork into cubes, cover with water and bring to a boil. Discard water. Fry pork cubes, add chicken livers and fry until done. Don't drain the fat from the salt pork. Add seasonings, onion and garlic. Put mixture through food processor. Add sherry and mix together. Spoon pâté into small containers. Serve with assorted crackers and breads. This freezes well. **Serves 8-10.**

CHOPPED CHICKEN LIVERS

Use this fresh pâté on Melba toast or dark rye bread with soups or as an appetizer with fresh breads.

1 lb.	chicken livers, chopped into small pieces	500 g
½ tsp.	grated garlic (optional)	2 mL
2	medium onions, chopped	2
⅓ cup	butter or chicken fat	75 mL
1 tsp.	salt	5 mL
½ tsp.	pepper	2 mL
3	eggs, hard-boiled, chopped	3

Sauté chicken livers, garlic and onions in butter. Do not brown. Add salt and pepper and cool. With a knife, coarsely chop liver and eggs and mix well in a bowl. If the mixture does not stick together, add more butter. Do not freeze. **Serves 6-8.**

BEER FONDUE

This is like a Welsh Rarebit in a pot. Use bread or vegetables for dipping.

2 cups	grated Swiss cheese	500 mL
2 cups	grated Cheddar cheese or Monterey Jack	500 mL
1 tbsp.	cornstarch	15 mL
½ tsp.	dry mustard	2 mL
1 tsp.	Worcestershire sauce	5 mL
2-3	drops hot pepper sauce	2-3
⅔ cup	beer	150 mL

Have cheese at room temperature. In a bowl, mix cheese, cornstarch and mustard. Toss to coat. Add Worcestershire and pepper sauces. Mix well. In a saucepan, heat beer until warm. Gradually add cheese mixture and stir constantly over medium heat until cheese melts. Quickly transfer to fondue pot and place over fondue burner. Spear a bread cube with a fondue fork, piercing the crust side last. Dip bread into cheese mixture. If the dip thickens, add a bit of warm beer. **Serves 6-8.**

VARIATION: Prepare a vegetable platter with broccoli, cauliflower, peppers, etc., and dip vegetables in the sauce. Choose cheese to suit your taste — use mild, medium or sharp.

Fondue Dippers

Many leftover foods make suitable dippers for fondue. Cut into bite-sized pieces, allowing 10-12 pieces for each person. Try French or Italian bread, hard rolls, bagels, bread sticks. Cut so that each piece has one side that is crust. Leftover cooked meat such as chicken, ham and seafood may also be used. Crisp vegetables make good dippers; try broccoli, carrots, mushrooms, cauliflower, peppers, celery, etc.

HOT & SPICY WINGS

3 lbs.	chicken wings (drumettes)	1.5 kg
½ cup	ketchup	125 mL
¼ cup	water	60 mL
¼ cup	honey	60 mL
¼ cup	red wine vinegar	60 mL
2 tbsp.	packed brown sugar	30 mL
1 tbsp.	Dijon mustard	15 mL
1 tbsp.	Worcestershire sauce	15 mL
1 tbsp.	soy sauce	15 mL
2 tbsp.	hot pepper sauce	30 mL
2	garlic cloves, minced	2
2 tbsp.	dried minced onion	30 mL

Remove tips from wings. If you wish, separate wings at the joint. Cover a broiler pan with foil and poke lots of holes in foil for drainage. Arrange chicken in a single layer and broil on both sides until lightly browned. Mix remaining ingredients in a saucepan and bring to a boil. Reduce heat and simmer for at least 5-10 minutes. With tongs, dip wings in sauce and replace on foil-covered broiler pan (or use a cookie sheet with a rim). Bake at 375°F (190°C) for 35-40 minutes. If desired, broil and crisp the wings. **Serves 8.**

GLAZED HONEY WINE MEATBALLS

Serve these very tasty meatballs as an appetizer or as a main course.

1	egg, beaten	1
3 tbsp.	milk	45 mL
1 tbsp.	Worcestershire sauce	15 mL
½ cup	bread crumbs	125 mL
1 lb.	hamburger, or a bit more	500 g
¼ cup	water	60 mL
¼ cup	red wine vinegar	60 mL
¼ cup	soy sauce	60 mL
1 tbsp.	cornstarch	15 mL
3-4 tbsp.	brown sugar, more if you like the sauce sweeter	45-60 mL
3 tbsp.	honey	45 mL
½ tsp.	ground ginger	2 mL
1-2	garlic cloves, grated or finely chopped salt to taste	1-2

In a large bowl, combine first 5 ingredients. Make into 1" (2.5 cm) balls. Place meatballs on greased rimmed cookie sheet and bake at 375°F (190°C) for 20 minutes, turning them as they bake. Make sauce while meatballs are baking. In a saucepan, blend together remaining ingredients. Bring to a boil. Put meatballs in casserole and pour sauce over them. Place casserole in oven and heat to boiling point. **Serves 6.**

SAUERKRAUT BALLS

Sauerkraut adds a bite to these appetizer or main course meatballs.

1 lb.	ground pork	500 g
1	medium onion, chopped	1
½ lb.	ground ham	250 g
½ cup	flour	125 mL
½ tsp.	dry mustard	2 mL
4	drops pepper sauce (optional)	4
½ cup	milk	125 mL
¼ cup	chopped parsley	60 mL
3 cups	sauerkraut, drained, washed, finely chopped	750 mL
⅓ cup	butter or margarine	75 mL
2	eggs	2
¼ cup	cold water	60 mL
¾ cup	bread crumbs	175 mL

SAUERKRAUT BALLS

Continued

Fry pork and onion until pork is cooked. Stir in ham, flour, mustard and pepper sauce. Stir in milk and cook over medium heat, stirring constantly, until hot, about 5 minutes. Stir in parsley and sauerkraut. Cool. Melt butter in a 9 x 13" (23 x 33 cm) pan. Beat together eggs and water. Shape pork into 1" (2.5 cm) balls. Dip balls in egg mixture and then in bread crumbs. Place in pan and bake for 30 minutes, turning once. Serve with a mustard sauce. **Makes about 50 appetizers.**

SPICED CRANBERRY PUNCH

This is great for skiing or skating parties.

1 cup	sugar	250 mL
4 cups	water	1 L
6	whole cloves	6
2	cinnamon sticks, about 3" (7 cm) long	2
8 cups	cranberry cocktail	2 L
2 cups	orange juice	500 mL
1/2 cup	lemon juice	125 mL
2 cups	dark rum	500 mL
1	orange, cut into thin slices	1
1	lemon, cut into thin slices	1

In a large pot, combine sugar, water, cloves, cinnamon sticks. Bring to a boil and simmer for 5 minutes. Cover and let cool. Strain punch mixture into a large punch bowl. Stir in cranberry cocktail, orange and lemon juice. Just before serving, add rum and stir. Add orange and lemon slices to the punch. Serve cold. **Serves 10-12.**

VELVETY SMOOTH EGGNOG

12	egg yolks	12
1½ cups	sugar	375 mL
12	egg whites	12
pinch	salt	pinch
5 cups	whole milk	1.25 L
4 cups	whipping cream	1 L
26 oz.	bourbon	750 mL
1 cup	rum	250 mL

Beat egg yolks with 1 cup (250 mL) sugar until very light. In a glass or stainless steel bowl, beat egg whites until frothy. Add salt and keep beating. Gradually add remaining ½ cup (125 mL) sugar and beat until stiff peaks form. Combine egg yolk and egg white mixtures. Whip whipping cream until stiff. Fold into egg mixture. Stir in bourbon, rum and milk. Make the eggnog a few days before you use it. Store in refrigerator in glass jars. Stir well before serving. **Serves 12.**

CAFÉ SUPRÊME

Serve this incredibly rich and delicious coffee instead of a dessert.

1 cup	coffee liqueur (Tia Maria or Kahlúa)	250 mL
½ cup	brandy	125 mL
½ cup	crème de cocoa	125 mL
½ cup	amaretto	125 mL
8 cups	hot strong coffee	3.5 kg
	whipped cream	
	chocolate or cinnamon	

Combine liqueurs in a pitcher. Put 3 or 4 tbsp. (45-60 mL) of liqueur mixture into each coffee cup. Fill cups with coffee, top with whipped cream and sprinkle with chocolate or cinnamon. **Serves 6.**

See photograph on page 175.

COUNTRY
FLAVORS

Soups

MAKING SOUP STOCKS

Good stocks are the most important ingredients for good soups. Make stocks ahead and freeze them.

	beef bones or chicken necks and backs	
1	large onion, chopped	1
2-3	garlic cloves, chopped	2-3
1-2	bay leaves	1-2
	salt and pepper	

Place beef bones or chicken necks and backs in large pot and cover with cold water. Bring to a boil for 5 minutes. Empty pot into sink and wash the pot and the chicken pieces or beef bones. Place bones in pot and cover with 4" (10 cm) of water. Add onion, garlic, bay leaves, salt and pepper. Simmer bones for 2 to 3 hours. If water boils down too much, just add more water. When stock is done, let it cool. Remove bones and strain broth. Cool and skim off fat. Divide broth into smaller portions. Freeze.

ONION SOUP

The browned beef bones add a wonderful rich flavor to this soup.

3	large beef soup bones	3
2 tbsp.	vegetable oil	30 mL
4 qts.	cold water, add more if it simmers down	4 L
2	bay leaves	2
4-5 cups	sliced onions	1-1.25 L
4 tbsp.	butter	60 mL
1 tsp.	sugar	5 mL
2 tbsp.	flour	30 mL
1	loaf French bread, in ½" (1.3 cm) slices	1
	grated cheese	

In a heavy 8-quart (8 L) soup pot, heat oil and brown the beef bones. Add water and bay leaves. Simmer for 2-3 hours. Strain. In a frying pan, combine onions, butter, sugar and flour. Stir onions until browned and carmellized, about 10 minutes. Put onions into soup pot and add 2 quarts (2 L) of beef stock, more as needed. Simmer for 20 minutes. Get onion soup bowls or a large casserole ready. Toast enough slices of bread to have 2 pieces of toast per serving. Place ½" (1.3 cm) thick bread slices on cookie sheet. Bake at 375°F (190°C), turn when toasted on 1 side, making sure it is dry. Put 1 slice of toast in bottom of soup bowl and sprinkle with cheese. Fill bowls to ¾ with hot onion soup and top with the second piece of toast. Cover toast with lots of cheese. Bake in 350°F (180°C) oven until cheese is melted and soup is hot, about 2-3 minutes. You will have some beef broth left over; it freezes well for the next time. **Serves 10.**

SOUPS & BREADS

LEEK SOUP

3	leeks	3
3 tbsp.	butter or margarine	45 mL
1	medium onion, sliced	1
1	garlic clove, minced	1
4	medium potatoes, diced	4
3 cups	chicken broth, page 50	750 mL
1	bay leaf	1
	salt and pepper to taste	
3 cups	creamilk (10% m.f.)	750 mL
¼ cup	chopped chives or green onions	60 mL

Wash leeks carefully, cut off most of the green and discard. Thinly slice the rest of the leeks. In a heavy pot, melt butter and add onion, garlic and sliced leeks. Sauté until soft. Add diced potatoes, chicken broth and bay leaf. Simmer for about 40 minutes over low heat. Remove bay leaf. Mash the potatoes with a potato masher, or purée in a food processor. Add salt, pepper and cream. Bring just to a boil. Serve with a sprinkle of chives or green onions. **Serves 6.**

POTATO & CABBAGE SOUP

My mother used to make this. Ukrainian recipes used a lot of cabbage. Farm cream (whipping cream) makes this rich and flavorful.

3 tbsp.	butter	45 mL
1	large onion, chopped	1
2	celery stalks, chopped	2
2-3 cups	shredded cabbage	500-750 mL
	salt and pepper	
3	medium potatoes, peeled and diced	3
1	large carrot	1
6-8 cups	chicken stock, page 50, heated	1.5-2 L
1 tbsp.	chopped fresh dill	15 mL
1 cup	whipping cream	250 mL
2 tbsp.	flour	30 mL
	sour cream for garnish	

In a large saucepan, heat butter and sauté onion. Add celery and cabbage and season well with salt and pepper. Add potatoes and carrot to chicken stock and simmer for 20-30 minutes, until they are done. Add dill and cream and simmer 5 minutes more. Add cabbage mixture to potato mixture. Add salt and pepper to taste. Mix flour with a bit of cold water and add to soup while it is simmering. If you wish, garnish with sour cream. **Serves 6.**

POTATO SOUP WITH DUMPLINGS

This hearty Ukrainian soup has dumplings that are like fat noodles.

4	large potatoes, diced very small	4
6-8 cups	chicken broth, page 50	1.5-2 L
1	medium carrot, sliced	1
1	medium onion, chopped	1
1	garlic clove, minced	1
2 tbsp.	butter	30 mL
	salt and pepper to taste	
1 tbsp.	dried parsley	15 mL
2	celery stalks, finely chopped	2
	parsley, chopped	
	green onions, chopped (optional)	

DUMPLINGS:

1	egg	1
1 tbsp.	water	15 mL
¾ cup	flour	175 mL
¼ tsp.	salt	1 mL

Combine first 9 ingredients in a soup pot; simmer for 40 minutes. Mix dumpling ingredients into a stiff dough, knead until smooth. Let rest for ½ hour or less. On a floured board, roll dough into a long thin roll and cut into bite-sized pieces. Add dumplings to soup, cover and simmer for 15 minutes. You may need to add more broth or water. Add parsley or green onions towards the last bit of cooking. **Serves 8.**

UKRAINIAN BORSCHT

This was a winter soup — traditionally made to use up the beets in the root cellar. Now we just make it because it's delicious.

2 lbs.	spare ribs	1 kg
10-12 cups	water	2.5-3 L
1	large onion, finely chopped	1
2-3	garlic cloves, finely chopped	2-3
1	bay leaf	1
6	medium-sized beets, grated	6
2	carrots, chopped	2
2 cups	white or broad beans, soaked overnight and boiled until tender	500 mL
½	small head of cabbage, shredded	½
	salt and pepper to taste	
14 oz.	can tomatoes, chopped	398 mL
1 tsp.	dried dill (optional)	5 mL
	sour cream	
	salted green onion, page 72	

UKRAINIAN BORSCHT

Continued

Place ribs in a large pot, cover with cold water and bring to a boil. Discard water; wash ribs and soup pot to remove all the scum. Return ribs to pot, add water, onion, garlic and bay leaf. Bring to a boil; simmer for at least an hour. Remove meat from the bones and return meat to broth. Add beets, carrots, beans and cabbage. Simmer until tender, about 1-1½ hours. Add salt, pepper, tomatoes and dill; simmer for a few minutes. Serve with a tbsp. (15 mL) of sour cream and a tsp. (5 mL) of salted green onions in each bowl. **Serves 12.**

NOTE: Do not add commercial sour cream to the soup pot, it will curdle. Add a spoonful of commercial sour cream to individual bowls.

FRESH VEGETABLE BORSCHT

This summer soup uses vegetables in season.

8	medium-sized beets, or more, cut crosswise into slices and shredded	8
2	large carrots, chopped	2
1 cup	fresh peas	250 mL
2 cups	string beans, cut into small pieces	500 mL
3 cups	shredded cabbage	750 mL
4	new potatoes (optional)	4
2	ripe tomatoes, chopped or 1 cup (250 mL) tomato juice	2
1	garlic clove, minced	1
	cold water	
5-6 cups	chicken broth	1.25-1.5 L
1	onion or 3 green onions, chopped	1
1 tbsp.	butter	15 mL
2 cups	whipping cream	500 mL
2 tbsp.	chopped fresh dill (optional)	30 mL
	chopped parsley	
	chopped chives to garnish	

In a large soup pot, combine first 8 ingredients. Add enough cold water to barely cover the vegetables. Bring to a boil, reduce heat and simmer until all vegetables are cooked, about 1½ hours. Add chicken broth, cook another 20 minutes. In a frying pan, sauté onion in butter just until soft. Add whipping cream and boil for 2-3 minutes. Pour creamed onions into the soup. Add dill if desired and parsley. Garnish bowls of borscht with chopped chives. **Serves 8.**

See photograph on page 51.

WILD RICE SOUP

¾ cup	wild rice	175 mL
6-8	slices bacon, chopped	6-8
1 cup	chopped celery	250 mL
1 cup	chopped onion	250 mL
½ cup	chopped green pepper (optional)	125 mL
2 cups	finely chopped mushrooms	500 mL
7-8 cups	chicken broth	1.75-2 L
1 cup	white sauce, page 122	250 mL
2	garlic cloves, finely chopped	2

Wash rice and boil for 20 minutes. Drain and set aside. Fry bacon until crisp. Remove bacon pieces, sauté onions, celery, green peppers and mushrooms in the bacon fat until just transparent. Add chicken broth and garlic and cook over low heat for 1 hour. Add cream sauce and simmer soup for 10 minutes. Garnish with a few fried sliced mushrooms, chopped chives or a sprinkle of green onion. **Serves 8.**

CLAM CHOWDER

4	large potatoes, peeled and chopped	4
1	large carrot, grated	1
2	celery stalks, chopped	2
4 cups	chicken broth or water	1 L
4-6 oz.	salt pork or bacon, finely diced	125-170 g
¼ cup	butter	60 mL
1	large onion, chopped	1
1	garlic clove, minced (optional)	1
	salt and pepper to taste	
3 x 5½ oz.	cans clams, drained	3 x 143 g
1 qt.	creamilk (10% m.f.)	1 L
1 tbsp.	dried parsley	15 mL
1	large ripe tomato, chopped (optional)	1

In a saucepan, combine potatoes, carrots and celery. Add enough chicken broth or water to just cover vegetables. Simmer vegetables for 30-45 minutes, until very tender. If using salted pork, cover pork with cold water and boil for about 5 minutes. Drain. In a frying pan, in 1 tbsp. (15 mL) butter, fry salt pork until crisp or use crisply fried bacon; add to cooked vegetables. Sauté chopped onion and garlic in remaining butter, add to vegetables. Add remaining ingredients, bring to a boil; simmer for 2-3 minutes.

VARIATIONS: For Fish Chowder, substitute 1 lb. (500 g) cod pieces for clams. For Creamed Corn & Clam Chowder, add a 19 oz. (540 mL) can of creamed corn to the Clam Chowder. Omit the tomatoes.

See photograph on page 51.

COUNTRY
FLAVORS

Salads
&
Salad
Dressings

OLD-FASHIONED SALADS

There was never any salad dressing on our farm, so my Mom improvised, as did everyone else. Mom would use sour cream or if the cream was sweet she would add vinegar. People will remember this salad. It is the basis of the ranch or farm dressing which is so popular today.

	sour cream or sweet (whipping) cream	
1 tsp.	**vinegar, if needed**	5 mL
	salt and pepper to taste	
2	**green onions**	2
	head or leaf lettuce, washed and torn	

If the cream is sweet add vinegar. Add salt and pepper. Place green onion and lettuce in a salad bowl and pour sour cream mixture on top. Toss and serve. **Serves 4.**

CUCUMBER & ONION SALAD

My Mom never put the salad in the refrigerator. It was made fresh and promptly eaten.

1 cup	**sour cream, see recipe above**	250 mL
½ tsp.	**sugar**	2 mL
	salt and pepper to taste	
2	**cucumbers, peeled, sliced**	2
1	**large onion, thinly sliced**	1
4	**radishes, thinly sliced**	4
3 tbsp.	**chopped green onion or chives**	45 mL

In a large bowl, combine cream, sugar, salt and pepper. Stir in the remaining ingredients. Refrigerate for ½ hour and serve. **Serves 4-6.**

NOTE: If you are using English cucumbers, do not peel.

VARIATION: We made Sour Cream Cucumbers as soon as we had fresh cucumbers in the garden. Add 1 tsp. (5 mL) of vinegar to the dressing above, use 1 red and 1 white onion and omit radishes. Add 1 tsp. (5 mL) chopped fresh dill if you wish. Refrigerate for 1 hour before serving.

CAESAR SALAD

1	medium head romaine lettuce	1

DRESSING:

2	garlic cloves, minced or grated	2
½ tsp.	salt	2 mL
4	anchovies, patted dry and chopped	4
½ tsp.	coarse black pepper	2 mL
2 tbsp.	lemon juice	30 mL
1 tbsp.	vinegar	15 mL
1 tbsp.	Dijon mustard	15 mL
1 tsp.	Worcestershire sauce	5 mL
¼ cup	olive oil	60 mL

FRIED CROÛTONS:

¼ cup	olive or salad oil	60 mL
2	garlic cloves, cut in half	2
4-5 cups	cubed Italian bread	1-2.5 L
½ cup	grated Parmesan cheese	125 mL

Wash lettuce leaves and dry between towels. Tear into large pieces. Put all ingredients for dressing, except olive oil, into blender. Blend until smooth, then slowly add oil. When oil is blended in, refrigerate until ready to make salad. To prepare the croûtons, heat oil and garlic in frying pan. When oil is hot, remove garlic and add cubed bread to oil. Stir and turn bread cubes while frying. The croûtons should be toasted on all sides. Cool before using. To make salad, toss lettuce with dressing until well-coated. Sprinkle with Parmesan cheese and add croûtons. Serve immediately. **Serves 6.**

VARIATION: For Baked Croûtons, I butter bread with garlic butter, cut it into cubes and toast it in the oven on a cookie sheet at 425°F (220°C). Watch carefully and stir once or twice.

HELPFUL HINT:

• Lettuce will keep longer if you don't wash it before you store it. Wash just before using.

SPINACH SALAD

1-2	bunches of spinach	1-2
1 cup	bean sprouts	250 mL
2	hard-boiled eggs, sliced	2
½ lb.	bacon, fried crisp and crumbled	250 g
5 oz.	water chestnuts, sliced (optional)	150 g
1	medium onion, thinly sliced	1

DRESSING:

½ cup	vegetable oil	125 mL
¼ cup	sugar	60 mL
¼ cup	ketchup	60 mL
½ tsp.	salt	2 mL
1 tsp.	Worcestershire Sauce	5 mL
¼ cup	cider vinegar	60 mL

Thoroughly wash and dry spinach and tear into bite-sized pieces. Combine dressing ingredients in a jar and shake well. Toss all salad ingredients together. Pour dressing over salad and serve immediately. **Serves 8.**

See photograph on page 123.

LAYERED SPINACH SALAD

1	small head of lettuce, torn	1
1-2 qts.	spinach, torn	1-2 L
1 cup	thinly sliced red or white onion rings	250 mL
1 cup	frozen peas, cooked and drained	250 mL
5	eggs, hard-boiled, sliced	5
1 cup	chopped celery	250 mL
½ cup	mayonnaise	125 mL
½ cup	sour cream	125 mL
½ tsp.	sugar	2 mL
	salt and pepper to taste	
1-1½ cups	grated Cheddar cheese (optional)	500-750 mL

Layer first 6 ingredients. Mix together mayonnaise, sour cream, sugar, salt and pepper. Pour over layered ingredients. Sprinkle with shredded Cheddar cheese (optional). **Serves 6.**

COLESLAW

1	firm head of cabbage, shredded	1
2	green onions, chopped	2
1	celery stalk, chopped	1
1	carrot, grated	1
½	red pepper, chopped (optional)	½
½	green pepper, chopped (optional)	½

COLESLAW DRESSING:

½ cup	mayonnaise	125 mL
¼ cup	plain yogurt or sour cream	60 mL
1 tbsp.	sugar	15 mL
1 tsp.	Dijon mustard	5 mL
1 tsp.	white vinegar	5 mL
	salt and pepper to taste	

In a large salad bowl, combine the coleslaw ingredients. To make the dressing, mix all ingredients together. Pour over cabbage mixture and refrigerate until ready to use. **Serves 8.**

CARROT SALAD

½ cup	mayonnaise	125 mL
1 tbsp.	sugar	15 mL
	salt and pepper to taste	
2-3 cups	grated carrots	500-750 mL
1 cup	diced celery	250 mL
1 cup	chopped red & green peppers (optional)	250 mL
½ cup	raisins, washed and dried	125 mL
½ cup	roasted, chopped peanuts, walnuts or pecans	125 mL

In a large bowl, combine mayonnaise, sugar, salt and pepper. Add the remaining ingredients. Toss together and chill until ready to serve. Serve with chicken, lamb or pork. **Serves 4-6.**

VARIATION: Add chopped, peeled oranges and/or toasted sunflower seeds.

APPLE SALAD

4	apples, any variety	4
1	celery stalk, diced	1
½ cup	broken pecans or walnuts	125 mL
½ cup	raisins, well-washed	125 mL
½ cup	mayonnaise	125 mL
1 tbsp.	sugar	15 mL
½ tsp.	salt	2 mL

Peel apples and cut into quarters. Chop each quarter into 3 pieces. Add celery, nuts and raisins. Combine mayonnaise, sugar and salt. Toss with the apple mixture. Add more mayonnaise if desired. Serve with pork chops, chicken, duck or goose. **Serves 4-6.**

VARIATION: Add whole or halved seedless green grapes.

See photograph on page 51.

BEET AND ONION SALAD

| 4 | beets, cooked | 4 |
| 1 | small red or white onion, thinly sliced | 1 |

DRESSING:		
2-3 tbsp.	red wine vinegar	30-45 mL
1 tsp.	sugar	5 mL
1 tbsp.	oil	15 mL
	salt and pepper to taste	
	lettuce leaves	
	parsley	

Slice cold beets and then cut into long thin pieces (julienne). Add sliced onion. Mix well. Combine all dressing ingredients. Toss gently with beets and onion. Arrange lettuce leaves on a plate and spoon beet salad into the lettuce cups. Sprinkle with fresh, chopped parsley. **Serves 6**.

VARIATION: Sprinkle hard-boiled egg, coarsely chopped, over the salad. This salad may also be layered in a bowl for serving. Try a tsp. (5 mL) of Dijon mustard added to the dressing.

WHITE & GREEN CAULIFLOWER

3 cups	each white and green cauliflower florets	750 mL
½ cup	chopped parsley	125 mL
1 tsp.	capers	5 mL
2	garlic cloves	2
2 oz.	anchovies	50 g
½ tsp.	orange zest	2 mL
¼ cup	olive oil	60 mL
2 tbsp.	lemon juice	30 mL

Arrange white and green cauliflower florets in bowl and sprinkle with parsley. Process remaining ingredients and pour over cauliflower. **Serves 8-10.**

RED & GREEN PEPPER SALAD

A colorful salad for Christmastime or on a hot summer day.

2	red peppers, thinly sliced into rings	2
2	green peppers, thinly sliced into rings	2
1	white onion, thinly sliced	1
1	red onion, thinly sliced	1
4	ripe tomatoes, cut in wedges or sliced	4
10	ripe olives, sliced	10
2 oz.	anchovies, drained, chopped (optional)	50 g

TARRAGON VINAIGRETTE DRESSING:

¼ cup	olive oil	60 mL
¼ cup	red wine vinegar	60 mL
2	garlic cloves, crushed	2
1 tsp.	salt	5 mL
½ tsp.	dried tarragon leaves	2 mL
	freshly grated pepper to taste	
1 tbsp.	chopped parsley	15 mL
2 tbsp.	chives or green onion	30 mL
1 tbsp.	sugar (optional)	15 mL

Prepare vegetables and anchovies for salad. Put all ingredients for dressing in a jar and shake well. Refrigerate until ready to use. In a shallow glass dish, layer the peppers and the two kinds of onions. Scatter tomatoes, olives and anchovies, if used, on top and pour dressing over. Or arrange sliced tomatoes on a deep platter and arrange remaining vegetables in the middle. **Serves 10.**

See photograph on page 17.

MIXED BEAN SALAD

Variations of this salad are indispensable for summer picnics and buffets.

14 oz.	kidney beans	398 mL
14 oz.	yellow waxed beans	398 mL
14 oz.	green beans	398 mL
1	medium onion, sliced	1
1	green pepper, sliced	1
1 cup	chopped celery	250 mL
¼ cup	vegetable oil	60 mL
½ cup	vinegar	125 mL
¼ cup	sugar	60 mL
1	garlic clove, grated	1
½ tsp.	salt	2 mL
	pepper to taste	

Rinse the beans and drain well. Add onion, green pepper and celery. Combine remaining ingredients and pour over beans. Refrigerate overnight. **Serves 12-14.**

WILD RICE SALAD

I have experimented with wild rice in many recipes. The soy sauce adds just the right touch to the dressing.

4 cups	cooked wild rice (1 cup [250 mL] raw)	1 L
4	radishes, sliced	4
4	green onions, chopped	4
1	carrot, shredded	1
4-5	olives, chopped (optional)	4-5
2	celery stalks, chopped	2
½	green pepper, chopped	½
½	red pepper, chopped	½
1 cup	mayonnaise	250 mL
2	garlic cloves, grated	2
2 tbsp.	soy sauce	30 mL
1 tsp.	salt	5 mL
½ tsp.	pepper	2 mL

WILD RICE SALAD

Continued

In a large bowl, combine rice and vegetables. Combine mayonnaise, garlic, soy sauce, salt and pepper; pour over rice and vegetables. Mix well and refrigerate for 2 hours before serving. **Serves 8-10.**

Variations: For Shrimp Wild Rice Salad, add 2 cups (500 mL) cooked small shrimp. Also try half brown rice. For Chicken or Turkey Wild Rice Salad, add 2 cups (500 mL) chopped cold cooked chicken or turkey.

See photograph on page 69.

RICE SALAD

People always phone me for this recipe. With extra shrimp this salad makes a whole meal.

1 cup	rice	250 mL
1 tsp.	salt	5 mL
2-3 cups	boiling water	500-750 mL
1 tbsp.	vegetable oil	15 mL
½ cup	finely chopped green onion	125 mL
½ cup	chopped olives	125 mL
½ cup	chopped celery	125 mL
1 or 2	4 oz. (113 g) tins of shrimp	1 or 2
2 tbsp.	Russian dressing	30 mL
2 tbsp.	mayonnaise	30 mL
	salt, pepper, cayenne to taste	
2-3	radishes, sliced (optional)	2-3

In a heavy pot, combine rice, salt and water. Boil rice, uncovered, for 10-15 minutes. Reduce heat and cover pot. Cook for 10-15 minutes longer. Turn off stove and let rice steam for half an hour. Empty rice into a bowl and gently mix oil into the rice. Cool. Mix together remaining ingredients and combine with cooled rice. Refrigerate to blend flavors before serving. **Serves 8.**

PASTA ARTICHOKE SALAD

5 cups	cooked pasta (shells, bows, fusilli, etc.)	1.25 L
1 tbsp.	vegetable oil	15 mL
1/2 cup	mayonnaise, or more	125 mL
4	garlic cloves, minced	4
1	lemon, juice of	1
1 tsp.	Dijon mustard	5 mL
1 tsp.	salt	5 mL
1/4 tsp.	pepper	1 mL
3	green onions, chopped	3
2 cups	torn spinach	500 mL
1 cup	red or green pepper strips	250 mL
1 cup	cooked green peas	250 mL
6 oz.	jar marinated artichoke hearts, drained	170 mL
1/2 cup	sliced green olives (optional)	125 mL

Cook pasta according to directions. Rinse in cold water and drain well. Toss with oil so pasta doesn't stick. Cool in refrigerator. Mix together mayonnaise, garlic, lemon juice, mustard, salt and pepper. Combine pasta and vegetables. Toss with dressing. Chill. **Serves 8.**

NOTE: If cooked pasta has stuck together, place in a colander and dip in boiling water.

CRANBERRY ORANGE SALAD

6 oz.	pkg. raspberry gelatin	170 g
1 cup	boiling water	250 mL
1 1/2 cups	cranberries, fresh or frozen	375 mL
1	celery stalk, diced	1
1	orange, peeled and chopped	1
1	apple, quartered and chopped	1
1/2 cup	chopped walnuts	125 mL

Prepare gelatin using 1 cup (250 mL) of boiling water. When gelatin has cooled, add remaining ingredients. Pour into a 6-cup (1.5 L) mold and refrigerate overnight. Unmold to serve. **Serves 6.**

TOMATO SHRIMP ASPIC

This recipe is lovely on a Christmas buffet and it is a refreshing summer lunch or dinner salad.

2 cups	tomato juice	500 mL
2 tbsp.	unflavored gelatin (2 env.)	30 mL
½ cup	cold water	125 mL
1 cup	mayonnaise	250 mL
4 oz.	pkg. cream cheese	125 g
1 cup	diced celery	250 mL
½ cup	diced green pepper	125 mL
½ cup	grated onion	125 mL
4 oz.	can of broken or small shrimp	113 g
½ cup	sliced stuffed green olives (optional)	125 mL

Heat tomato juice. Dissolve gelatin in cold water and add to heated tomato juice. Cool. Cream mayonnaise and cream cheese together and add to cooled tomato juice. Add vegetables and shrimp. Pour into a 6 cup (1.5 L) mold or deep bowl which has been lightly oiled. Leave overnight in the refrigerator. Unmold to serve. **Serves 8.**

VINAIGRETTE DRESSING

6 tbsp.	red wine vinegar	90 mL
1½ tbsp.	Dijon mustard	22 mL
1½ tsp.	sugar	7 mL
¾ tsp.	salt	3 mL
¼ tsp.	pepper	1 mL
¼ cup	olive or vegetable oil	60 mL
1	garlic clove, grated	1

Put all ingredients in small jar and shake. Store in refrigerator. **Makes about ¾ cup (175 mL) of dressing.**

SOY WHISKY DRESSING

2 tbsp.	soy sauce	30 mL
1 tbsp.	vegetable oil	15 mL
1 tbsp.	rye whisky	15 mL
½ tsp.	sugar	2 mL
½ tsp.	tarragon	2 mL
	salt and pepper to taste	

Put all ingredients in a small jar and shake. Use for sliced onions, sliced cucumbers and tomato salads. **Makes ¼ cup (60 mL).**

FRENCH DRESSING

⅓ cup	vegetable or olive oil	75 mL
½ cup	vinegar, white or cider	125 mL
1 tsp.	salt	5 mL
¼ tsp.	pepper	1 mL
½ tsp.	sugar	2 mL
1	garlic clove, grated	1

Combine all ingredients in a screw-top jar. Shake. **Makes about 1 cup (250 mL) of dressing.**

VARIATION: Try blueberry or raspberry vinegar or lemon juice instead of white vinegar.

LEMON MUSTARD VINAIGRETTE

3 tbsp.	lemon juice	45 mL
1 tbsp.	prepared mustard	15 mL
1	garlic clove, grated	1
½ tsp.	dried tarragon	2 mL
2 tbsp.	olive or vegetable oil	30 mL
	salt and pepper to taste	

Combine first 4 ingredients and gradually whisk in oil. Add salt and pepper. Store in a jar in refrigerator. **Makes about 7 tbsp. (90 mL).**

POPPY SEED DRESSING

1 cup	liquid honey	250 mL
1 tsp.	salt	5 mL
½ cup	vinegar	125 mL
¾ cup	vegetable oil	175 mL
½	small onion, grated	½
1 tsp.	dry mustard	5 mL
2 tsp.	poppy seeds	10 mL

Place all ingredients in a jar; shake to blend. Refrigerate. Shake before using. Use on fruit or vegetable salads. **Makes about 2½ cups (625 mL).**

Baked Whole Trout, page 96
Wild Rice Salad, page 64
Cornmeal Muffins, page 23

COUNTRY
FLAVORS

Vegetables
&
Side Dishes

SALTED GREEN ONIONS

These preserved onions are a French tradition. When you are thinning out green onions in the garden, preserve them in salt to use as a garnish.

| 4 or 5 | bunches of green onions | 4 or 5 |
| ½ cup | coarse pickling salt | 125 mL |

Chop onions into small pieces. Put them in a bowl. Add pickling salt and mix. Store in refrigerator in a jar. These onions keep for months. They make a great addition to soup. Add ½-1 tsp. (2-5 mL) to individual servings. **Makes about 1 cup (250 mL).**

MUSHROOM SAUTÉ

1 lb.	mushrooms	500 g
3 tbsp.	butter (heaping)	45 mL
1	medium onion, sliced	1
2	garlic cloves, crushed	2
2 tbsp.	soy sauce	30 mL
	salt and pepper to taste	

Slice mushrooms if they are large. Leave small ones whole. In a frying pan, heat butter to very hot. Add onions and mushrooms. Stir over low heat, add garlic, soy sauce, salt and pepper. Serve with chicken, steak or pork chops. **Serves 6.**

BAKED ZUCCHINI WITH CHEESE

3-4	small zucchini, sliced	3-4
1	small onion, sliced	1
1 cup	grated Cheddar cheese	250 mL
	salt and pepper to taste	

Butter a 9 x 13" (23 x 33 cm) casserole, layer zucchini, onion and cheese. Season to taste. Bake at 350°F (180°C) for 30 minutes. **Serves 4-6.**

VARIATION: Add a layer of sliced tomatoes, a finely grated garlic clove and a sprinkle of thyme and oregano. Layer cheese last.

SPINACH SQUARES

This is a nice light supper dish. It is like a quick, no-crust quiche.

2 x 10 oz.	pkgs. frozen chopped spinach	2 x 283 g
3 tbsp.	butter or margarine	45 mL
1	onion, chopped	1
2 cups	sliced mushrooms	500 mL
5	eggs	5
1 cup	white sauce, page 122	250 mL
½ cup	grated Parmesan or Cheddar cheese	125 mL
½ cup	bread crumbs	125 mL
	salt and pepper to taste	
¼ tsp.	dried basil or oregano leaves	1 mL

Thaw spinach and press out all water. In a frying pan, melt butter and sauté onion and mushrooms just until onion is limp. Add spinach. Beat eggs, add white sauce, 3 tbsp. (45 mL) of cheese and crumbs; mix well. Combine with the spinach mixture. Add salt, pepper and basil or oregano. Pour spinach mixture into a greased 9" (23 cm) square pan. Cover with remaining cheese. Bake at 350°F (180°C) for 40-50 minutes. Cut into squares and serve hot with cold meat and garlic bread. **Serves 4-6.**

FRENCH-FRIED ZUCCHINI

4	small zucchini	4
⅓ cup	flour	75 mL
1 tsp.	salt	5 mL
2	eggs	2
2 tbsp.	water	30 mL
1 cup	flour	250 mL
½ cup	grated Parmesan cheese	125 mL

Trim ends of zucchini and cut into strips like large French fries. Combine ⅓ cup (75 mL) flour and salt. Beat eggs with water. Combine 1 cup (250 mL) flour with cheese. Roll zucchini pieces in flour and salt mixture, dip in eggs and roll in flour and cheese mixture. Deep-fry at 375°F (190°C) until golden, about 3-4 minutes. Drain on paper towels. **Serves 4-6.**

GREEN BEANS & BACON

6	slices bacon, cut in small pieces	6
1	onion, chopped	1
2-3 cups	green beans, sliced diagonally	500-750 mL
1/4 cup	toasted, sliced almonds	60 mL

Fry bacon pieces until crisp. Add onion and sauté. Grease an 8" (20 cm) square casserole and put in beans. Top beans with bacon and onions and sprinkle with toasted almonds. Heat at 350°F (180°C) for 20 minutes or until hot. **Serves 3-4.**

VARIATIONS: Use frozen French-style green beans or canned green beans when fresh beans are not available.

See photograph on page 105.

BEANS, BEANS, BEANS

For a large crowd you can multiply this quick and tasty recipe.

1/2 lb.	bacon	250 g
1 cup	chopped onions	250 mL
14 oz.	can green beans, drained	398 mL
14 oz.	can lima beans, drained	398 mL
14 oz.	can pork and beans	398 mL
14 oz.	can kidney beans, drained	398 mL
1/2 cup	packed brown sugar	125 mL
1/3 cup	vinegar	75 mL
1/4 cup	molasses	60 mL
1/3 cup	ketchup	75 mL
1 tsp.	minced garlic	5 mL
1/2 tsp.	dry mustard or 1 tsp. (5 mL) prepared	2 mL
1/4 tsp.	pepper	1 mL

Cut bacon into small pieces; fry until brown and crisp. Remove bacon and discard about half of fat. Sauté onion in remaining fat. In a large pot, combine remaining ingredients with bacon and onion. Heat in oven for 30-40 minutes at 350°F (180°C). **Serves 8-10.**

MOM'S BAKED BEANS

When my son, Ray, owned "Little Acres Barbecue" I made at least 60 gallons (240 L) of these beans a week. They were very popular with everyone.

2	pieces salt pork or bacon, each about 6" (1.5 cm) square	2
6 cups	dried beans (I use Thompson's) water	1.5 L
3 tbsp.	lard	45 mL
38 oz.	fancy molasses (1⅓ lbs.)	675 g
2 cups	ketchup, more if desired	500 mL
½ cup	lard	125 mL
1 tbsp.	dry mustard	15 mL

Cut pieces of salt pork into thick slices, cover with cold water and boil for 3-4 minutes. This will remove some of the salt. Discard water. You do not have to parboil bacon. Wash beans and remove any bad ones. Put beans in a 6-quart (6 L) Dutch oven or heavy roaster. Cover with lukewarm water, to a depth of 4-5" (10-13 cm) above the beans. Soak overnight. In the morning, add 3 tbsp. (45 mL) of lard and boil beans for 1 hour or more. Beans are done when they begin to split, or bite 1 to check doneness. Remove from heat. Add molasses, ketchup, ½ cup (125 mL) lard and mustard. Mix gently, the mixture should be sloppy. Add parboiled salt pork. Do not salt beans when you are cooking them, this toughens the beans. Put beans in oven and bake, uncovered, at 400°F (200°C) for 1 hour. Reduce heat to 275°F (140°C) or 300°F (150°C) and bake for 3-4 hours longer. Cover the beans after they brown. Baking will reduce the water so you might have to add more water or tomato juice. Also taste for salt and pepper. If you use salt pork you might not have to salt the beans. **Serves 16-18.**

See photograph on the front cover.

FRIED CABBAGE

8	slices bacon, diced	8
1	large onion, chopped	1
1	medium cabbage, shredded	1
½ tsp.	salt	2 mL

In a skillet, fry diced bacon and chopped onion until onion is tender, about 6-7 minutes. Add shredded cabbage and salt. Fry for 10 minutes, or until cabbage is tender. **Serves 4.**

RED CABBAGE AND APPLES

¼ cup	butter or margarine	60 mL
2	apples, peeled and sliced	2
1	onion, chopped	1
1	medium head red cabbage, shredded	1
1 cup	water	250 mL
½ cup	red wine vinegar	125 mL
½ cup	brown sugar	125 mL
1 tsp.	salt	5 mL
	pepper to taste	

In a large heavy pot, melt butter and sauté apple and onion for 10 minutes, or until tender. Add cabbage, water, vinegar, sugar, salt and pepper. Reduce heat to low and cover. Simmer for 30 minutes. Serve with roast pork or pork chops. **Serves 4-6.**

CABBAGE ROLLS

Buy cabbage in the fall when cabbage is cheaper and the selection is better. That's, of course, if you have a deep freeze. Select cabbage that is soft and the leaves are loose. It's so much easier to separate the leaves. Blanch the cabbage before freezing it. Cut at least 2" (5 cm) from the root end of the cabbage. With a sharp knife take out some of the core. I use a canner and fill it ⅔ with water. When the water is almost boiling, add the cabbage, 1 or 2 at a time. With a long fork, turn the cabbage and take off individual cabbage leaves. Do not allow the water to boil. Have the sink filled with cold water and quickly cool the leaves. If you have a double sink use both. Put the leaves in a colander and drain. At this time you could trim out the center vein and cut the leaves to desired size. Put leaves in plastic bags, in flat stacks, and freeze. When you are ready to make cabbage rolls, take out a package and put in cold or warm water to thaw.

Cabbage Rolls — Rice Filling

Whipping Cream Sauce, below, or Tomato Sauce is good with these.

2 cups	pearl or short-grain rice	500 mL
1 tbsp.	salt	15 mL
4 cups	boiling water	1 L
1	large onion, finely chopped	1
½ cup	butter or margarine, or more	125 mL
	salt and pepper to taste	
	cabbage leaves	
10 oz.	can tomato soup plus 1 can of water	284 mL
	or 20 oz. (570 mL) tomato juice	

In a heavy saucepan, combine rice and salt. Pour boiling water over rice and stir over high heat until it starts to boil. Cover rice, reduce heat and cook for 8-10 minutes. Shut off the heat and let rice steam for 20 minutes. Do not overcook rice. Sauté onions in butter. Scoop rice into a large bowl and add sautéed onion. Add salt and pepper to taste. When rice is cool, make cabbage rolls. Put 1 tbsp. (15 mL) of filling mixture at the base of cabbage leaf. Fold in sides and roll up leaf. Put cabbage rolls, seam side down, in a 4-quart (4 L) casserole and add tomato juice or tomato soup just to cover, OR add sautéed onion and whipping cream, see below. Bake at 350°F (180°C) for 2-2½ hours. Reduce heat to 275°F (140°C) and bake for another hour. You may need more sauce; if so add juice or water. **Serves 6-8.**

Cabbage Rolls with Whipping Cream

Use this sauce only on the plain rice cabbage rolls.

1 tbsp.	butter or margarine	15 mL
1	large onion, finely chopped	1
2-3 cups	whipping cream	500-750 mL
	salt and pepper to taste	

In a large frying pan, melt butter and sauté onion just until soft. Add whipping cream, salt and pepper to taste. Heat but do not boil; pour creamed onions over cabbage rolls. See above for baking instructions You may have to add more cream as the cabbage rolls bake.

See photograph on page 87.

Cabbage Rolls — Buckwheat Filling

My mother made this Ukrainian recipe often. We also used a lot of buckwheat in casseroles.

2 cups	buckwheat	500 mL
5-6 cups	water	1.25-1.5 L
½ lb.	bacon, finely chopped	250 g
1	large onion, finely chopped	1
2 tsp.	salt	10 mL
	pepper to taste	
6 tbsp.	butter or bacon fat	90 mL
1	onion, chopped, sautéed	1
4 tbsp.	butter or margarine, melted	60 mL

Spread buckwheat over a cookie sheet with edges. Put in 275°F (140°C) oven to roast, being careful to stir often. It should take about ¾ hour. Put buckwheat into a pot; pour boiling water over it; cook and stir until it starts to boil. Reduce heat; cover and cook until the water is reduced, about 10 minutes. In a large skillet, fry bacon pieces until crisp. Add onion and sauté but do not brown. Mix together with buckwheat, salt, pepper and butter or bacon fat. When cool make cabbage rolls, see page 77. Add water, just to cover, to the casserole, instead of tomato juice. Top with sautéed onions and melted butter before baking. See baking instructions on page 77. **Serves 6-8.**

See photograph on page 87.

Cabbage Rolls — Hamburger and Rice

Tomato sauce is the best with these cabbage rolls.

	Rice Filling, page 77	
1 tbsp.	butter or margarine	15 mL
1 lb.	ground pork or beef	500 g
1	large onion, chopped	1
1-2	garlic cloves, grated (optional)	1-2
1 tbsp.	dried parsley	15 mL
	salt and pepper to taste	

In a large frying pan, melt butter and fry ground meat and onion until onions are soft and meat is no longer pink, but not browned. Add garlic, parsley, salt and pepper to taste. Add to rice and mix together. Cool rice mixture and make cabbage rolls, see page 77. **Serves 8-10.**

CORN CUSTARD

This baked corn dish is good with steak, pork or chicken.

¼ cup	butter or margarine	60 mL
1	medium onion, chopped	1
¼ cup	chopped green pepper (optional)	60 mL
½ cup	bread and/or cracker crumbs	125 mL
2	eggs, beaten	2
½ cup	milk	125 mL
15 oz.	can creamed corn	425 mL
½ tsp.	salt	2 mL
	pepper to taste	

Melt butter in frying pan. Sauté onions, green pepper and bread crumbs. Beat eggs with milk; add to corn. Add onion mixture and salt and pepper. Pour into a 2-quart (2 L) casserole and bake for 45-60 minutes at 350°F (180°C), until set. When you insert a knife in the center and it comes out clean, it's done. **Serves 4-6.**

VARIATIONS: Use kernel corn and ¼ cup (60 mL) cream instead of creamed corn, add red pepper for color and, if you wish, add some heat with red pepper flakes or Cajun spice.

NACHYNKA

My mother often made this recipe and added pork cracklings.

1	medium onion, finely chopped	1
1 cup	butter or margarine	250 mL
1 cup	cornmeal	250 mL
1 tsp.	sugar	5 mL
1 tsp.	salt	5 mL
1 qt.	warm milk	1 L
4	eggs, well-beaten	4
1 tsp.	baking powder	5 mL

Sauté onion in butter. Do not brown. Add cornmeal, sugar, salt and warm milk. Cook, stirring until cornmeal thickens. Remove from heat; add eggs and baking powder. Pour into a well-greased 4-quart (4 L) casserole and bake at 325°F (160°C) for 1½ hours. Serve hot. **Serves 6-8.**

VARIATION: If you want to add ¼ lb. [125 g] crisply fried, crumbled bacon, use chicken broth instead of milk.

See photograph on page 87.

CORNMEAL CASSEROLE

This Ukrainian casserole is related to the Italian Polenta and Southern Cornmeal Mush. It is good with Fried Chicken with Cream, page 99.

3 cups	boiling water	750 mL
1 tsp.	salt	5 mL
¾ cup	cornmeal, or a bit more	175 mL

In a pot, bring water to a boil, add salt and slowly add cornmeal. Continue stirring until thickened. Pour into a greased 2-quart (2 L) casserole and bake about 30 minutes at 350°F (180°C). **Serves 6.**

PEROGIE DOUGH

This is very good perogie dough. Beating the eggs produces a lighter dough.

1	egg	1
¼ cup	oil	60 mL
1 tsp.	salt	5 mL
1 cup	lukewarm water	250 mL
4 cups	flour	1 L
1 tbsp.	salt	15 mL
	melted butter	

Beat egg until light. Add oil, salt and water. Add flour and mix with your hands. This should make a soft dough. Cover with waxed paper and let rest for ½ hour. On a floured counter, roll to ⅛" (3 mm) thickness. Cut dough into 3" (7 cm) circles. Fill with your favorite filling. Put 1 tsp. (5 mL) of filling in the middle of the dough. Fold dough in half and pinch edges together to seal. Have a large pot half full of boiling water, add 1 tbsp. (15 mL) of salt. Add perogies to boiling water. After perogies rise to the top, boil for 8 to 10 minutes. Have melted butter ready. Put perogies in a bowl and pour melted butter over them. Serve hot. If you wish, serve perogies with crumbled crisp bacon, sautéed onions and sour cream. **Makes 60-70 perogies.**

NOTE: To freeze, line a cookie sheet with waxed paper and put perogies in a single layer. Put in freezer. When frozen, put perogies into plastic bags and seal.

Cheese Filling for Perogies

10-12	large potatoes, peeled	10-12
1	onion, finely chopped	1
2-3 tbsp.	butter	30-45 mL
1½ cups	grated Cheddar cheese	375 mL
	salt and pepper to taste	

Boil potatoes; drain and leave pot on the stove to dry potatoes. Mash potatoes without milk. Sauté onion in butter. Do not brown. Add grated cheese and onion to the hot mashed potatoes and mix until cheese is melted. Cool potato mixture in a bowl. Add more cheese if you like. Add salt and pepper to taste. Use as filling for perogie dough. **Makes 60-70 perogies.**

VARIATION: Use 2 cups (500 mL) cottage cheese instead of Cheddar cheese. Add to cold potatoes.

See photograph on page 87.

Sauerkraut Filling

1 qt.	sauerkraut	1 L
1½ cups	water	375 mL
6-8	bacon strips, finely chopped	6-8
1	medium onion, finely chopped	1

In a saucepan, combine sauerkraut and water. Boil for about 20 minutes. Drain and squeeze sauerkraut dry. Chop medium fine. Fry bacon until crisp. Remove bacon and sauté onion in bacon fat until translucent. Combine bacon, onion and sauerkraut. Cool. Use as a filling for perogie dough. **Makes 30-40 perogies.**

See photograph on page 87.

VEGETABLE HINTS:

- To keep cauliflower white, add 2 tbsp. (30 mL) of milk to the cooking water.

- When boiling corn, add 1 tbsp. (15 mL) of sugar instead of salt. The corn will toughen if you add salt.

- To ripen tomatoes, put them in a brown paper bag and put in a dark place.

- When cooking vegetables grown below ground (potatoes, carrots, parsnips, turnips), place in cold water to cook. Place vegetables grown above ground, in boiling water to cook.

ROAST POTATOES

4 tbsp.	butter or margarine	60 mL
3	garlic cloves, grated	3
½ tsp.	salt	2 mL
¼ tsp.	pepper, or to taste	1 mL
12	or more small potatoes, peeled	12

Combine butter, grated garlic, salt and pepper. Rub each potato with garlic butter and put into a 9 x 13" (23 x 33 cm) greased pan. Bake, uncovered, at 375°F (190°C) to 400°F (200°C) for 1 hour. Stir the potatoes while baking so that they brown all over. Reduce heat if potatoes brown too much. **Serves 4.**

See photograph on the front cover.

POTATO DUMPLINGS (GNOCCHI)

These Italian dumplings are also very good with any pasta sauce.

6	large potatoes, boiled and mashed	6
1 cup	flour, more if needed	250 mL
1 tsp.	salt	5 mL
1	egg	1
2 tbsp.	oil	30 mL
1	onion, chopped	1
2	garlic cloves, grated	2
1 cup	finely chopped broccoli	250 mL
2 cups	grated carrots	500 mL

Put the warm mashed potatoes into a bowl. Add flour, salt and egg. Mix together and knead gently. Turn potato dough onto floured counter and knead, adding more flour if needed. Take piece of dough and roll into a finger-thin roll. Cut each roll into 1" (2.5 cm) pieces. When all the dough is cut into pieces, drop gnocchi into a pot of salted boiling water. Boil for 10 minutes. After the dough rises to the top of the water, stir gently with a wooden spoon. Drain well. In a frying pan, heat oil, add onion, garlic, broccoli and carrots; sauté briefly, keeping vegetables very crisp. Put Gnocchi on a large platter. Pour the vegetables over the Gnocchi. **Serves 6.**

POTATO PANCAKES

This recipe is Ukrainian, German and Jewish. Needless to say, it is very good.

4 cups	grated potatoes, drained	1 L
1 tsp.	salt	5 mL
3	eggs, beaten	3
½ cup	flour	125 mL
	pepper to taste	
	butter or vegetable oil	

Combine potatoes, salt, eggs, flour and peppers; mix well. Pan fry individual pancakes in hot fat until browned on both sides, about 4-5 minutes. Serve with sour cream, cottage cheese or applesauce. **Serves 6.**

WILD RICE POTATO PATTIES

2-3 tbsp.	butter or vegetable oil	30-45 mL
1	medium onion, chopped	1
2 cups	cold mashed potatoes	500 mL
1 cup	cooked wild rice, see below	250 mL
	salt and pepper to taste	

In a frying pan, heat 1 tbsp. (15 mL) butter and sauté onion. In a bowl, combine mashed potato, wild rice, sautéed onion, salt and pepper. Mix well and shape into patties. Melt remaining butter in pan and fry patties until browned on both sides. Served with fish or cold meat. **Serves 4.**

WILD RICE

I find that when I soak wild rice for 1 hour, it cooks faster. Wash 1 cup (250 mL) of wild rice by letting water run through it in a colander. Cover wild rice with warm water and let soak for 1 hour. Discard soaking water. Add wild rice to 3-4 cups (750 mL-1 L) of cold water. Boil for 40-50 minutes. I always cook wild rice about 10 minutes longer for salads. For casseroles, the rice will be baking and needs less cooking time. Brown rice can be cooked with wild rice. They take the same amount of time to cook.

SWEET POTATO, FRUIT & NUTS

My friend Daria makes this recipe every Easter and it's delicious. She varies the amount of nuts and raisins. This is not a recipe but a "put together." Vary ingredients and amounts to suit your taste.

2	medium sweet potatoes	2
2	Golden Delicious apples, peeled, sliced	2
1 cup	dark raisins	250 mL
1 cup	sunflower seeds	250 mL
3/4 cup	brown or yellow sugar	175 mL
1/2 tsp.	each ginger, cinnamon and nutmeg	2 mL
1/2 cup	melted butter	125 mL
1/2 cup	sweetened flaked coconut	125 mL
1 cup	cashew nuts or pecans	250 mL

In a saucepan, in salted water, cook potatoes about 40 minutes. Peel and cut into slices. Layer potatoes, apples, raisins and sunflower seeds. Mix together sugar, spices, butter, coconut and nuts and sprinkle over each layer. Keep some nuts and coconut to sprinkle on top layer. Cover with a double layer of foil and bake at 350°F (180°C) for about 1 hour. **Serves 10.**

See photograph on page 105.

BUCKWHEAT AND BACON CASSEROLE

Another of my mother's recipes, bacon adds a rich smoky flavor to this Ukrainian dish. Serve with roast pork or chicken.

1/2 lb.	bacon, finely chopped	250 g
1	large onion, chopped	1
3 cups	chopped mushrooms	750 mL
2 cups	buckwheat grits	500 mL
5 cups	chicken broth, page 50	1.25 L
1 1/4 cups	white sauce, page 122	300mL

BUCKWHEAT AND BACON CASSEROLE

Continued

Fry bacon until crisp. Remove from pan and add onions and mushrooms. Fry until soft. In a large pot, combine buckwheat and chicken broth. Bring to a boil, stirring. Cover pot and reduce heat, cook for 20 minutes. Shut off heat and let the buckwheat steam for 30 minutes. Grease a 4-quart (4 L) casserole. Place half of the cooked buckwheat in casserole. Mix bacon and mushrooms with cream sauce and put half of the mushroom mixture over the buckwheat. Add remaining buckwheat. Top with the rest of the bacon and mushroom sauce. Add garlic to mushroom mixture if you like. Bake at 350°F (180°C) for 1 hour, or until heated through. **Serves 8-10.**

WILD RICE & SPINACH CASSEROLE

A wonderful combination of layered vegetable flavors.

1½ cups	wild rice, washed	375 mL
2 cups	chicken broth, page 50	500 mL
1 bunch	spinach or 10 oz. (283 g) frozen	1 bunch
8 oz.	cream cheese, at room temperature	250 g
	salt to taste	
2 cups	chopped mushrooms	500 mL
1	medium onion, chopped	1
4 tbsp.	butter or margarine	60 mL
½ cup	chicken broth	125 mL

Cook rice in 2 cups (500 mL) chicken broth for about 1 hour. In a separate pan, cook spinach until tender, 2-3 minutes; drain well. Combine cream cheese and spinach, add salt. Sauté mushrooms and onions in butter until golden. In a buttered 4-quart (4 L) casserole, layer ½ wild rice, ½ spinach, ½ mushrooms and onions. Repeat layers. Pour ½ cup (125 mL) chicken broth over all. Cover and bake at 350°F (180°C) for 1 hour. **Serves 8-10.**

VARIATION: Try chopped leftover vegetables, broccoli, cauliflower, carrots, etc., and 1 or 2 minced garlic cloves, substitute frozen mixed vegetables for the spinach. You could also use half wild rice and half brown rice.

BROWN & WILD RICE STUFFING

4 cups	cooked brown and wild rice	1 L
1 cup	grated carrots	250 mL
½ cup	raisins, washed	125 mL
1	apple, shredded	1
½ cup	chopped almonds	125 mL
pinch	thyme	pinch
	salt & pepper to taste	
1	large onion, chopped	1
4 tbsp.	butter or margarine	60 mL
½ cup	white wine	125 mL

Combine cooked rice, carrots, raisins, apple, almonds, thyme, salt and pepper. Sauté onion in butter until soft and add to rice mixture with wine. Mix well. Use as a stuffing for domestic duck, wild duck, Cornish hens, goose or pork chops. **Stuffs 2 ducks or 1 goose.**

VARIATION: Bake, covered, at 350°F (180°C) for 30-40 minutes, until vegetables are tender, and serve as a side dish. **Serves 4-6.**

ORANGE & PECAN WILD RICE STUFFING

1 cup	wild rice	250 mL
2 cups	water	500 mL
1 cup	orange juice	250 mL
1	large onion, chopped	1
1 cup	chopped celery	250 mL
½ cup	butter or margarine	125 mL
	salt and pepper to taste	
½ cup	raisins, washed	125 mL
½ cup	pecans or almonds	125 mL
1	orange, peeled & chopped	1

Cook rice in water and orange juice for 50 minutes. Sauté onion and celery in butter. Add to cooked rice and season with salt and pepper. Mix in raisins, nuts and orange pieces. Use to stuff domestic or wild duck. **Stuffs 2 ducks or 1 goose.**

VARIATION: Bake as a side dish to serve with chicken, pork or duck. **Serves 4-6.**

Nachynka, page 79
Cheese Perogies, page 81
Sauerkraut Perogies, page 81
Rice Cabbage Rolls with Whipping Cream, page 77
Buckwheat Cabbage Rolls, page 78
Cheese Nalysnyky, page 9

COUNTRY
FLAVORS

Entrées

CHEESE SOUFFLÉ

	flour or grated cheese	
4 tbsp.	butter	60 mL
4 tbsp.	flour	60 mL
1½ cups	milk	375 mL
	salt and pepper to taste	
⅛ tsp.	cayenne (optional)	0.5 mL
1 cup	grated mozzarella, Gruyère or Cheddar cheese	250 mL
5	egg yolks, beaten until light	5
5	egg whites at room temperature, beaten until stiff	5

Grease an 8-cup (2 L) casserole and sprinkle with flour or cheese. In a heavy pot, melt butter, add flour and mix well. Add cold milk and stir until sauce bubbles for 2-3 minutes. Add salt, pepper and cayenne. Remove from stove and slowly add cheese and beaten egg yolks. Fold in beaten egg whites. Pour into prepared casserole and bake at 350°F (180°C) for 50-60 minutes. Serve immediately. **Serves 6.**

MACARONI & CHEESE

Sautéed onion adds a wonderful flavor to this family favorite.

4 cups	elbow macaroni	1 L
3 tbsp.	butter	45 mL
¼ cup	finely chopped onion	60 mL
2 tbsp.	flour	30 mL
½ tsp.	salt	2 mL
¼ tsp.	pepper	1 mL
1½ cups	milk	375 mL
2 cups	grated Cheddar cheese	500 mL
	cheese for topping	

Cook macaroni according to package directions. Don't overcook. Drain. In a saucepan, melt butter and cook onion but don't brown. Stir in the flour, salt and pepper. Add milk all at once and cook while stirring until thickened. Add cheese and stir until melted. Pour over macaroni and turn into a 3-quart (3 L) casserole. Sprinkle additional cheese on top and bake at 350°F (180°C) for 40 minutes. **Serves 6.**

QUICK TOMATO GARLIC SAUCE

This tasty low-fat pasta sauce is ready in minutes.

1 tbsp.	olive oil	15 mL
1	medium onion, chopped	1
2-3	garlic cloves, minced	2-3
1 tsp.	crushed hot red pepper flakes (optional)	5 mL
1 tsp.	oregano	5 mL
1 tsp.	parsley	5 mL
1 tsp.	pepper	5 mL
1	green pepper, chopped	1
2 cups	tomato sauce	500 mL

Heat oil and sauté onion, garlic and pepper flakes for 5 minutes. Add the rest of the ingredients and simmer for 15 minutes. Serve over pasta. **Serves 4-6.**

VARIATION: Add 1 cup (250 mL) sautéed mushrooms. For a quick Meat Sauce, add this basic tomato sauce to 1 lb. (500 g) of drained sautéed hamburger. Simmer for a few minutes to blend flavors.

NOTE: 1 lb. (500 g) of pasta serves 4.

PASTA WITH PESTO

This version of a traditional Mediterranean recipe has much less oil.

1/2 cup	chopped fresh basil	125 mL
1/4 cup	chopped fresh parsley	60 mL
1/2 cup	grated Parmesan cheese	125 mL
1/4 cup	pine nuts, walnuts or almonds	60 mL
2	garlic cloves, minced	2
1/4 cup	olive or vegetable oil	60 mL
	salt to taste	
1 lb.	pasta	500 g

Place basil, parsley, cheese, nuts and garlic in food processor and blend together. Add oil slowly. Mixture should be like soft butter. This can be frozen. Cook pasta according to package direction. Toss pesto with hot pasta. **Serves 4**

PASTA, BACON AND VEGETABLE TOSS

This is a quick, nutritious dinner menu. Everyone loves pasta.

1 lb.	spaghetti, cooked	500 g
10	slices of bacon, each cut into 4 pieces	10
4 tbsp.	olive or vegetable oil	60 mL
1	onion, chopped	1
2-3	garlic cloves, minced	2-3
2 cups	small broccoli florets	500 mL
1	large carrot, cut into thin strips	1
1 cup	sliced mushrooms (optional)	250 mL
½	red or green pepper, cut in large pieces (optional)	½
	salt and pepper to taste	
½ cup	grated Parmesan cheese	125 mL

Cook spaghetti or your favorite pasta, following directions on package. Drain. Fry bacon until crisp, drain off fat. In a pan, heat oil and add onion and garlic. Do not brown. Add the rest of vegetables and stir-fry just until the vegetables are hot and tender crisp. Season with salt and pepper. Add bacon to vegetables. Serve spaghetti on a large platter. Pour vegetables and bacon over pasta and toss together. Sprinkle with cheese. **Serves 4.**

CREAMY SEAFOOD SAUCE

3 tbsp.	butter	45 mL
1	onion, chopped	1
2	garlic cloves, minced	2
2 cups	sliced mushrooms (optional)	500 mL
2 cups	whipping cream	500 mL
½ cup	dry white wine (optional)	125 mL
½ tsp.	Tabasco sauce	2 mL
	salt and pepper to taste	
2 tbsp.	flour	30 mL
2 x 5 oz.	cans baby clams, drained	2 x 142 g
2 x 4 oz.	cans shrimp	2 x 113 g
2 x 4 oz.	cans crab meat	2 x 113 g
1½-2 lbs.	linguini or your favorite pasta	750 g-1 kg
¼ cup	chopped fresh parsley or green onion	60 mL
½ cup	grated Parmesan cheese	125 mL

CREAMY SEAFOOD SAUCE

Continued

In a heavy saucepan, melt butter and sauté onion and garlic. Be sure the garlic does not brown. Add mushrooms, cream, wine, Tabasco sauce, salt and pepper. Boil for about 5 minutes to reduce the cream and thicken slightly. Mix flour with cold water and add to the sauce. Cook until the sauce thickens. Add clams, shrimp and crab meat to sauce, heat until it bubbles. Cook linguini or your favorite pasta to directions on package. Serve pasta on a large platter. Top with seafood sauce. Sprinkle parsley and cheese on top of pasta. **Serves 6-8.**

SPICY SHRIMP PASTA

1½ lbs.	pasta	750 g
2 tbsp.	oil	30 mL
1 lb.	fresh shrimp, peeled and deveined	500 g
28 oz.	can tomatoes and juice	796 mL
3	garlic cloves, minced	3
½ cup	chopped onion	125 mL
1 tbsp.	finely chopped ginger root (optional)	15 mL
1 tsp.	brown sugar	5 mL
½ tsp.	dried chili flakes	2 mL
¼ cup	chopped fresh parsley	60 mL

Cook pasta according to package directions. In a frying pan, heat oil and fry shrimp for 3-5 minutes. Remove shrimp to a bowl. To pan, add tomatoes, garlic, onion, ginger, sugar and chili flakes. Simmer over low heat for 20 minutes, until thick. Mash tomatoes with a fork. Add shrimp and heat through. Put pasta on a large platter and pour sauce over. Sprinkle parsley on top. Serve with a salad and garlic bread. **Serves 6.**

NOTE: Ginger can be added in large chunks and removed before serving, if you prefer.

LASAGNE ROLL-UPS

A new version of lasagne, this is versatile. It can be halved very easily, just bake in a smaller pan; make 4 or 6 if you prefer.

1 tbsp.	oil	15 mL
1 lb.	ground beef	500 g
1	large onion, chopped	1
2	garlic cloves, minced	2
1 cup	sliced mushrooms	250 mL
2-3 cups	spaghetti sauce*	500-750 mL
	salt and pepper to taste	
12	lasagne noodles, cooked	12
2 cups	cottage cheese	500 mL
10 oz.	pkg. frozen chopped spinach	283 g
1 cup	grated Parmesan cheese	250 mL

Heat oil in a saucepan, add ground beef, onion, garlic and mushrooms. Cook until hamburger is no longer red. Add spaghetti sauce and simmer for 10 minutes. Add salt and pepper to taste. Pour half the sauce into a 9 x 13" (23 x 33 cm) casserole. Spread each noodle with sauce, cottage cheese and spinach. Roll up noodles. Place in casserole and pour the remaining sauce over the noodles. Sprinkle Parmesan cheese on top. Bake at 375°F (190°C) for 50-60 minutes. **Serves 6.**

* Use your favorite sauce, or if in a hurry use a commercial sauce.

PORK-STUFFED CANNELLONI

Originally this dish was made with veal or lamb but I prefer the flavor of this version with ground pork.

½ lb.	cannelloni	250 g
1 lb.	ground pork	500 g
2 tbsp.	oil	30 mL
1	large onion, chopped	1
1 cup	chopped celery	250 mL
1	carrot, grated	1
2	garlic cloves, or more, grated	2
1 cup	bread crumbs	250 mL
2	eggs, beaten	2
1 tsp.	salt	5 mL
½ tsp.	pepper	2 mL
1 tsp.	dried savory	5 mL
1 tbsp.	dried parsley	15 mL
2 cups	tomato sauce	500 mL
1 cup	grated mozzarella or Cheddar cheese	250 mL

PORK-STUFFED CANNELLONI

Continued

Cook cannelloni according to directions on package. Do not overcook. Sauté ground pork in oil together with onion, celery, carrot and garlic for 10 minutes, or until done. Put in a bowl to cool. Add bread crumbs, beaten eggs, salt, pepper, savory and parsley. Mix together with your hands. Stuff cooked cannelloni with meat mixture. Put cannelloni into a greased 9 x 13" (23 x 33 cm) pan. Pour tomato sauce over and bake for 40 minutes. Remove from oven and sprinkle with cheese. Bake for 20 minutes longer. Serve with a salad and garlic bread. **Serves 4-6.**

VARIATION: Substitute ground lamb for pork. Use Cannelloni sheets for easy preparation.

MARINADE FOR SALMON

½ cup	soy sauce	125 mL
¼ cup	white wine	60 mL
2 tbsp.	vegetable oil	30 mL
1	garlic clove, grated	1
1 tsp.	sugar	5 mL
	salt and pepper to taste	
6	salmon steaks	6

Mix all marinade ingredients together, put in a plastic bag. Put salmon in bag. Do not skin the salmon. Be sure and put the plastic bag in a bowl to prevent dripping. Shake the bag to be sure all pieces are marinating. Marinate for 1-2 hours. Barbecue salmon over medium heat or bake at 350°F (180°C) for about 20 minutes for salmon steaks. Brush salmon with marinade while it's cooking. **Serves 6.**

BAKED SALMON OR TROUT

My son, Ray, who ran a large catering business near Edmonton, always baked salmon this way. It is absolutely delicious. He now has a You-Fish trout operation on his farm at Stony Plain. The trout we photographed were pulled from the lake just an hour before the photograph was taken.

14-16 lb.	whole salmon or several large trout	6-7 kg
5	layers of aluminum foil	5
1	lemon	1
	salt and pepper	
1	onion, thickly sliced	1
¼ lb.	butter	125 g

Clean and wash salmon, dry with paper towels. Lay salmon on a large well-buttered piece of foil. Squeeze lemon juice over salmon; season cavity and outside with salt and pepper. Fill cavity with onion, chopped lemon and butter. Fold foil so that no steam escapes; use 5 layers of foil, crisscrossed to seal in juices. Lay salmon in charcoal and bake 15 minutes per side. Let the salmon rest for 15-20 minutes before unwrapping. Or bake in the oven at 400-425°F (200-225°C) for 35-45 minutes. **Serves 18-20.**

VARIATION: Stuff trout with Crab or Shrimp Stuffing, page 97. Bake as above.

See photograph on page 69.

PAN-FRIED FISH

Sometimes the simplest recipes are the best.

1 lb.	fillets, fresh or frozen	500 g
1	egg	1
2 tbsp.	water	30 mL
⅔ cup	fine bread crumbs or flour	150 mL
2-3 tbsp.	butter or shortening for frying	30-45 mL

Thaw fish if frozen. Dry on paper towels. Beat egg with water; dip pieces of fish to coat both sides. Roll in bread crumbs or flour. Fry fish for about 6-7 minutes. Fish will be done when both sides are browned and crisp. Place fried fish on paper towel to absorb fat. **Makes 3 servings.**

LOBSTER CASSEROLE

Adaptable and delicious for a special lunch or light supper.

4 tbsp.	butter	60 mL
1/2 tsp.	dry mustard	2 mL
1 cup	sliced mushrooms	250 mL
1/2 cup	chopped onions	125 mL
1 cup	whipping cream	250 mL
3	egg yolks	3
1/4 cup	sherry (optional)	60 mL
1 tsp.	salt	5 mL
dash	cayenne	dash
2 x 4 oz.	cans lobster or shrimp	2 x 113 g

In a frying pan, melt butter; sauté mustard, mushrooms and onions until onions are soft, not browned. In a double boiler, heat cream and beaten egg yolks, stirring constantly. Add sherry, salt and cayenne. In a greased 2-quart (2 L) casserole, arrange lobster, mushrooms and onions. Pour egg mixture over all. Bake at 350°F (180°C) for 20-25 minutes. Serve with a wild rice casserole, pages 85, 86 or in pastry cups with a salad. **Serves 4.**

VARIATION: If fresh lobster is available use that of course. For Scallop Casserole use 1 lb. (500 g) scallops. You can pipe or spoon mashed potatoes around the edge of the casserole and sprinkle with 1/2 cup (125 mL) Gruyère or other cheese.

CORNISH HENS WITH CRAB STUFFING

4	cornish hens	4
	salt and pepper to taste	
	garlic powder to taste	
	paprika to taste	

Crab or Shrimp Stuffing:

1/2 cup	butter	125 mL
1	garlic clove, grated	1
1/2 cup	finely chopped onions	125 mL
1/2 cup	finely chopped celery	125 mL
1/4 cup	parsley	60 mL
4 oz.	can crab meat, squeezed dry, or shrimp	113 g
1 cup	bread crumbs	250 mL
1/2 tsp.	salt	2 mL
1/4 tsp.	pepper	1 mL
	melted butter for basting	

CORNISH HENS WITH CRAB STUFFING

Continued

Sprinkle hens with salt, pepper, garlic powder and paprika inside and out. Heat butter in a pan and sauté garlic, onion and celery until soft. Add rest of the ingredients and mix well. If you find that the dressing is a bit dry, moisten with 2 tbsp. (30 mL) water or milk. Stuff hens and tie the legs together. Place in a roasting pan; brush with melted butter and roast at 350°F (180°C) for 1-1½ hours. **Serves 4.**

NUT-STUFFED CHICKEN BREASTS

4	chicken breasts	4
½ cup	grated Cheddar cheese	125 mL
½ cup	chopped walnuts or pecans	125 mL
½ cup	fine bread crumbs	125 mL
2 tbsp.	chopped onion	30 mL
½ tsp.	salt	2 mL
	pepper to taste	
½ cup	flour	125 mL
4 tbsp.	butter	60 mL
½ cup	chicken broth or milk	125 mL
½ cup	white wine	125 mL
1 tsp.	chopped parsley	5 mL

Bone chicken breasts and pound to ¼" (1 cm) thickness. In a bowl, combine cheese, nuts, bread crumbs, onion, salt and pepper. Mix thoroughly. Put about 2 tbsp. (30 mL) filling on each chicken breast. Fold meat over filling and fasten with toothpicks. Roll stuffed chicken breasts in flour and fry in butter until light brown on all sides. Place chicken in a 9 x 13" (23 x 33 cm) casserole. In a frying pan, combine chicken broth and wine. Let boil over high heat until reduced and thick. Add parsley. Pour over chicken and bake for 20 minutes at 350°F (180°C). Serve with scalloped potatoes and Caesar salad. **Serves 4-6.**

FRIED CHICKEN WITH CREAM

When we made this recipe on the farm we had to catch the chickens first.
We also had to run to the well to bring up the cream from cold storage.

3 tbsp.	butter	45 mL
3 lb.	frying chicken, cut up	1.5 kg
½ tsp.	salt	2 mL
	pepper to taste	
1	medium onion, chopped	1
3 cups	whipping cream	750 mL
1 tbsp.	chopped dillweed	15 mL

In a frying pan, melt butter and add chicken pieces. Sprinkle with salt and pepper. When chicken is lightly browned, place pieces in a 4-quart (4 L) casserole and bake at 350°F (180°C) for 20-30 minutes. In same frying pan, sauté onion in remaining butter, add whipping cream and bring to a boil for 3-4 minutes. Add dill. Pour over chicken and bake for 20-30 minutes. Serve with Cornmeal Casserole, page 80. **Serves 6.**

STEWED CHICKEN & DUMPLINGS

3-4 lb.	stewing chicken, cut up	1.5-2 kg
6-8 cups	water	1.5-2 L
1 tsp.	salt	5 mL
	pepper to taste	
2	celery stalks, chopped	2
2	carrots, chopped	2
1	onion, chopped	1
3 tbsp.	each, flour and water	45 mL

DUMPLINGS:

1 cup	flour	250 mL
2 tsp.	baking powder	10 mL
1	egg, beaten	1
2 tbsp.	oil	30 mL
2 tbsp.	parsley	30 mL
¼ -½ cup	milk	60-125 mL

Put stewing chicken into a Dutch oven and cover with water. Add salt, pepper, celery, carrots and onion. Bring chicken to a boil; reduce heat and simmer for 2-3 hours. Let chicken cool in the broth. When cool, remove chicken. Discard fat, skin and bones; return cut-up meat to the broth and heat. Stir flour into water and add to chicken broth to thicken. Combine all dumpling ingredients and mix well. Drop by spoonfuls into boiling chicken and cover. Let simmer for 15 minutes. Do not remove lid while dumplings are steaming. Arrange chicken, vegetables and dumplings on a deep platter. Enjoy. **Serves 6.**

CHICKEN PIE

3 lb.	frying chicken, cut up	750 g
	salt and pepper to taste	
2	cooked carrots, chopped	2
1 cup	peas	250 mL
1 cup	chopped celery	250 mL
1 tbsp.	butter	15 mL
1	onion, chopped	1
1 cup	chopped mushrooms	250 mL
2 tbsp.	each flour and water	30 mL

Put chicken pieces into a large pot and just cover with water. Add salt and pepper to taste. Bring to a boil and simmer for 1 hour. Remove chicken to cool and reserve cooking broth. Remove meat from the bones and place in a 4-quart (4 L) casserole. Add carrots, peas and celery. In a frying pan, melt butter and sauté onion and mushrooms until limp. Add to vegetables in casserole. Combine flour and water, add to 1½ cups (375 mL) of simmering broth. Simmer until thickened. Pour over meat and vegetables. Top with biscuits or Cream Cheese Crust and bake, uncovered, for 1 hour at 350°F (180°C). **Serves 6-8.**

VARIATION: Use leftover turkey or use 1½-2 lbs. (750 g-1 kg) ground or cubed beef. Add 2 diced potatoes & 1 minced garlic clove.

Biscuits

2 cups	flour	500 mL
1 tbsp.	baking powder	15 mL
1 tsp.	salt	5 mL
1 tsp.	sugar	5 mL
2 tbsp.	butter or margarine	30 mL
1 cup	milk, or more	250 mL

Combine flour, baking powder, salt and sugar. Add butter and work as for pie crust. Add milk and knead just to mix dough together. Pat dough out on a floured board and cut into biscuits. Arrange on top of chicken and bake according to instructions above.

Cream Cheese Crust

8 oz.	cream cheese	250 g
½ cup	butter or margarine	125 mL
2½ cups	flour	625 mL
½ tsp.	salt	2 mL

Have cheese and butter at room temperature. Mix thoroughly. Mix in flour and salt. Wrap in waxed paper and refrigerate for 1 hour or more. When pie is ready to bake, roll out crust and fit over chicken mixture. Cut holes in crust for steam to escape and bake as instructions above.

CHICKEN LIVER AND PEPPERS

This quick and easy supper dish is very tasty with noodles.

3 tbsp.	butter or margarine	45 mL
1 lb.	fresh chicken livers	500 g
1	medium onion, chopped	1
3	garlic cloves, minced	3
1/2 tsp.	paprika	2 mL
1/2 cup	chopped green pepper	125 mL
1/2 cup	chopped red pepper	125 mL
6	mushrooms, chopped	6
1 lb.	noodles, cooked	500 g

In a frying pan, melt butter and sauté livers, onion, garlic and paprika. Cook just until livers are no longer pink. Add peppers and sauté for 3-4 minutes, so vegetables are cooked but still crisp. Put noodles on a hot platter and top with liver and vegetables. **Serves 4.**

SAUTÉED CHICKEN LIVERS

Fresh chicken livers are great in this Teriyaki stir-fry.

1/2 lb.	chicken livers	250 g
3 tbsp.	teriyaki sauce	45 mL
1 tbsp.	chopped parsley	15 mL
1	onion, chopped	1
2	garlic cloves, minced	2
3 tbsp.	butter	45 mL
1	small zucchini, sliced	1
8	pea pods	8
2	celery stalks, sliced	2
6	mushrooms, sliced	6
2 tbsp.	oil	30 mL
	salt and pepper to taste	
1/8 tsp.	paprika or to taste	0.5 mL
	rice, pasta or toast	

Marinate chicken livers in bowl with teriyaki sauce, parsley, onion and garlic. Let stand while you prepare vegetables. Sauté marinated chicken livers in butter with onion, garlic and parsley until just done, about 4-5 minutes. Don't overcook. In another pan, sauté vegetables in oil until cooked but still crisp. Season with salt, pepper and paprika. Mix with liver and serve on a platter of rice, pasta or toast. **Serves 6.**

WILD DUCK

The duck recipe you use depends on the hunter. If the duck is not badly damaged, I clean it and use it to roast with bread or wild rice dressing. If you have only saved the duck breasts, this mushroom and onion sauce gives the duck a lovely flavor.

4 tbsp.	butter or margarine	60 mL
4 or 6	duck breasts	4 or 6
2 tbsp.	flour	30 mL
1	onion, chopped	1
1 cup	sliced mushrooms	250 mL
1	garlic clove, minced	1
1 tsp.	salt, or more to taste	5 mL
	pepper to taste	

WHITE SAUCE:

2 tbsp.	flour	30 mL
2 tbsp.	butter	30 mL
2 cups	milk	500 mL
½ tsp.	salt	2 mL
	pepper to taste	

WILD RICE DRESSING:

4 tbsp.	butter or margarine	60 mL
1 lb.	sausage meat	250 g
1	onion, chopped	1
1 cup	cooked wild rice	250 mL
1 cup	cooked long-grain or pearl rice	250 mL
2	celery stalks, chopped	2
2 tbsp.	parsley	30 mL
1 tsp.	salt	5 mL
½ tsp.	pepper	2 mL

In a frying pan, melt 2 tbsp. (30 mL) butter. Dredge duck breasts in flour; fry for about 20 minutes on each side. Remove from frying pan; put into a 3-quart (3 L) casserole. Take the other 2 tbsp. (30 mL) of butter and sauté onion, mushrooms and garlic. Season with salt and pepper. Add to duck. To make the white sauce, combine the flour and butter over medium heat. Add milk. Stir until it thickens. Add salt and pepper; pour over duck and mushrooms. Bake in oven at 375°F (190°C) for 40 minutes. To make the dressing, in a frying pan, melt the butter and sauté the sausage for 5 minutes, breaking it up. Add the onion and fry until it is soft. In a bowl, combine remaining ingredients. Add meat mixture to rice and mix well. This is enough dressing to stuff 2-3 birds. You could use all wild rice if you like. Rub ducks with butter, salt and pepper. Roast, uncovered, at 375°F (190°C) for the first ½ hour. Reduce heat to 325°F (160°C) and roast for an additional hour. **Serves 4.**

NOTE: If you are in a hurry, instead of white sauce use a 10 oz. (284 mL) can mushroom soup with 1 soup can of milk.

ROAST DUCK

4-5 lb.	duck	2-2.5 kg
1 tsp.	salt	5 mL
1	large onion, chopped	1
2	garlic cloves, minced	2
2	unpeeled oranges, quartered	2
	salt and pepper to taste	
	Orange Sauce, recipe below	

Wash duck and wipe with paper towel. Sprinkle salt in cavity. Place duck in a shallow pan or roaster. Fill cavity with onion, garlic and oranges. Sprinkle salt and pepper on duck to taste. Roast at 375°F (190°C), uncovered, for 1½ hours. Prick the duck all over with a fork, so the fat drains as the duck roasts. Cover duck and roast at 325°F (160°C) for 1 more hour. When duck is done, cut up and put on hot platter. Pour hot Orange Sauce over duck. Serve with rice or a wild rice casserole, page 85, 86. **Serves 3-4.**

Orange Sauce

1½ cups	chicken broth	375 mL
½ cup	orange juice	125 mL
1 tbsp.	tomato paste	15 mL
1 tsp.	grated garlic	5 mL
1 tbsp.	flour	15 mL
⅓ cup	burgundy	75 mL
3 tbsp.	brandy	45 mL
2 tbsp.	grated orange rind	30 mL
1	orange, peeled, sectioned (optional)	1
2 tbsp.	orange marmalade	30 mL
¼ cup	brown sugar for a sweeter sauce	60 mL

In saucepan, combine chicken broth, orange juice, tomato paste and garlic and bring to a boil. Reduce heat. Mix flour with a bit of water and thicken the chicken broth. When thick, add burgundy and brandy. Boil for a minute and add grated orange rind, orange sections, orange marmalade and sugar, if using. Pour sauce over roast duck slices. **Makes about 3 cups (750 mL) of sauce.**

See photograph on page 105.

BREADED PORK TENDERLOIN

1 lb.	pork tenderloin, cut crosswise into 6 pieces	500 g
½ cup	flour	125 mL
1 tsp.	seasoned salt	5 mL
¼ tsp.	pepper	1 mL
1	egg, beaten	1
2 tbsp.	milk	30 mL
1 cup	fine dry bread crumbs	250 mL
1 tsp.	paprika	5mL
3 tbsp.	shortening	45 mL
¾ cup	chicken broth	175 mL
1 tbsp.	flour	15 mL
½ cup	sour cream	125 mL

Pound pork tenderloin until thin. Combine flour, seasoned salt and pepper. Coat meat with flour mixture. Combine egg and milk. Dip each cutlet into milk mixture, then into crumbs mixed with paprika. In a large skillet, heat shortening and fry cutlets for 3-4 minutes. Remove from pan and keep hot. To make sauce, pour broth into skillet. Combine the flour and sour cream. Stir the sour cream mixture into the broth. Cook, stirring until thick. Serve with pork. **Serves 4.**

PORK MARINADE

This marinade is great with a roast and with strips or cubes of pork to be barbecued.

2-3	garlic cloves, crushed	2-3
3 tbsp.	soy sauce	45 mL
2 tbsp.	brown sugar	30 mL
2 tbsp.	black bean sauce	30 mL
1 tbsp.	sesame oil	15mL
2 tsp.	sliced ginger root	10 mL
½ cup	wine (red or white)	125 mL
4-5-lb.	pork roast or smaller	2-2.2 kg

Mix all ingredients, except pork, in a bowl. Pour into a plastic bag and put the roast in the marinade. Put bag and roast in a large bowl. Refrigerate and marinate overnight.Turn roast often in bag to marinate all sides. Take roast out of marinade; discard marinade. Place roast and ½ cup (125 mL) of water in a roasting pan. Roast at 350°F (180°C) for 2-3 hours. **Serves 6-8.**

VARIATION: Marinate cubes or strips of pork overnight. Thread pork strips or cubes onto skewers and broil 6-8 minutes.

Roast Duck with Orange Sauce, page 103
Sweet Potato, Fruit & Nuts, page 84
Green Beans & Bacon, page 74

TOURTIÉRE

My sister-in-law, Lucienne, shared this old family recipe with me. It is a traditional French Canadian dish.

2 lbs.	lean ground pork	1 kg
1	medium onion, finely chopped	1
1	garlic clove, finely chopped	1
½ tsp.	salt	2 mL
½ tsp.	savory	2 mL
¼ tsp.	cloves	1 mL
¼ tsp.	cinnamon	1 mL
1 cup	water, or more	250 mL

PASTRY:

3 cups	flour	750 mL
½ lb.	lard	250 g
1 tsp.	salt	5 mL
½ tsp.	baking powder	2 mL
1	egg, beaten	1
1 tsp.	vinegar	5 mL
½ cup	cold water	125 mL
¾ cup	fine bread crumbs	175 mL
1	egg, beaten	1
1 tbsp.	water	15 mL

In a large pot, combine all filling ingredients, bring to a boil and simmer for 30-40 minutes. Skim off the fat as the meat cooks. Adjust spices to suit your taste. To make pastry, work flour, lard, salt and baking powder with your hands until well-mixed. Mix together beaten egg, vinegar and ½ cup (125 mL) water. Add to flour mixture and mix until it forms a ball. This should be enough pastry for 2, 9" (23 cm) pies. Roll out pastry to fit pie plate. Sprinkle crumbs on bottom of crust and then pour in the cooked meat. Cover with top pastry, cut steam vents and brush with 1 egg beaten with 1 tbsp. (15 mL) water. Bake at 350°F (180°C) for 30-40 minutes. **Makes 2, 9" (23 cm) pies.**

PORK HOCK RAGOÛT

This is my sister-in-law Lucienne's recipe. There are many variations for this prized French Canadian dish. This is the way I made it for my family. You can serve it with or without tiny meatballs.

2-3	pork hocks, about 1½ lbs. (750 g)	2-3
1	large carrot, cut up	1
1	medium onion, chopped	1
1	bay leaf	1
	salt and pepper to taste	
1	garlic clove, halved	1
½ cup	flour, browned	125 mL
¼-½ cup	cold water	60-125 mL
	tiny meatballs (optional), page 109	
⅛ tsp.	cinnamon (optional)	0.5 mL
⅛ tsp.	cloves (optional)	0.5 mL

Wash pork hocks and put in a large kettle. Add enough cold water to cover pork hocks. Bring to a boil and boil for 3-4 minutes. Take pot off the stove and empty it into the sink. Wash hocks and clean the pot. Put pork hocks back into clean kettle and add enough water to cover them. Add the carrot, onion, bay leaf, salt, pepper and garlic clove. Cover and simmer for 2½-3 hours. Be sure to add a bit more water if it is reduced. Remove pork hocks from stock and strain the stock. Remove the meat from the bones and return meat and stock to the pot. In a heavy frying pan, over medium heat, add flour, stir until light brown. Cool flour and mix with cold water to make a thin paste. Add to the ragoût to thicken the stock. Add meat balls, cinnamon and cloves if you wish. Bring ragoût to a boil and set aside. You could serve ragoût as is or with plain boiled potatoes and a salad. This freezes well and is always handy to have for a quick meal. **Serves 8-10 people.**

Tiny Meatballs

1½-2 lbs.	ground pork	750 g-1 kg
1	garlic clove, minced	1
½ tsp.	salt	2 mL
	pepper to taste	
⅛ tsp.	allspice (optional)	0.5 mL
1	slice of bread, soaked in water, squeeze out moisture	1
1	egg, beaten	1
1 tbsp.	butter or margarine	15 mL

In a bowl, combine pork, garlic, salt, pepper, allspice, bread and egg. Shape into small balls using approximately 1 tsp. (5 mL) of meat for each meatball. In a frying pan, heat butter, add meatballs and brown. Add to ragoût. You may need more salt and pepper.

STUDENETZ

This Ukrainian specialty is for Jellied Pork Hocks and Pigs Feet. Slice and serve for lunch with good rye bread and mustard. This is also nice with potato salad.

4-5	pieces of pork hocks	4-5
1	pig's foot (to make pork hocks jell)	1
4	garlic cloves, chopped	4
1	bay leaf	1
1	carrot, cut into chunks	1
2	celery stalks, chopped	2
	salt and pepper to taste	
1	large onion, cut in half	1

In a large kettle, place the washed pork hocks and pig's foot, cover with cold water and bring to a boil. Remove the scum. Empty the pot into the sink. Wash pot and pork hocks and foot. Return meat to the kettle and just cover with clean water, no more. Arrange meat evenly in the pot. Slowly bring to a boil. Skim off all the scum. Let hocks simmer slowly. This will give a clear broth. Add remaining ingredients and simmer for about 3 hours. The meat should fall off the bones. The liquid will be reduced. Take hocks out of liquid and put on a tray. Cool; cut meat into chunks. The skin could be chopped finely and mixed with the meat. Put chopped meat into a large bowl. Taste broth to check seasoning. Strain broth over meat and mix. If you have too much liquid, do not use it all. Put meat mixture into a 9" (23 cm) square pan to jell. Refrigerate. Remove any fat that settles on top of the meat. **Serves 8-10.**

MARINADE FOR PICKLED PORK HOCKS

When I was a child we ate pork hocks with sauerkraut or made jellied pork hocks. This recipe is a new way of serving pork hocks.

4-5	**fresh pork hocks**	4-5
8 qts.	**water**	8 L
1 lb.	**pickling salt**	500 g
1 tsp.	**saltpeter**	5 mL
2	**garlic cloves, minced**	2
1	**large onion, chopped**	1
2	**carrots, chopped**	2
1 cup	**chopped celery**	250 mL
2	**bay leaves**	2
2 tbsp.	**whole allspice in a cheesecloth**	30 mL

In a large pot, make brine for pork hocks by bringing water, salt, and saltpeter to a boil. Boil for 3 minutes. Let cool. Wash and scrape pork hocks and put into a 4-quart (4 L) crock or glass jug. Pour brine over pork hocks and let stand in refrigerator for 10 days. Move pork hocks often to be sure that they are covered with brine. Take pork hocks out of brine after 10 days. Put in a large pot and cover with cold water. Bring to a boil and boil for 5 minutes. Remove pork hocks and put them in a pot with garlic, onion, carrot, celery, bay leaf and allspice. Cover pork hocks to 2/3 with water, and boil for about 3 hours. Discard cooking broth. Serve pork hocks with sauerkraut. **Serves 4-6.**

Sauerkraut

1 qt.	**sauerkraut**	1 L
8-10	**pieces of bacon, diced**	8-10
1	**onion, chopped**	1
1	**potato, grated**	1
1 cup	**water**	250 mL

Wash sauerkraut if too sour. Fry bacon pieces, until cooked but not crisp. Combine all ingredients in a buttered 3-quart (3 L) casserole and bake at 350°F (180°C) for 1½ hours. Serve on a large platter with pickled pork hocks. **Serves 4-6.**

CIPÂTE

In this layered meat pie, inexpensive cuts of meat are made tender and flavorful with this long-cooking method. The gravy soaks into the double crust and gives it a lovely rich flavor. Traditionally this French Canadian meat pie was made with a mixture of wild game. Substitute venison or duck or pheasant if you like. My Uncle Joe used to make this meat pie and my version came from watching him.

5-6 lb.	chuck steak or chuck roast, cut into small chunks	2.2-2.5 kg
3	large onions, sliced	3
3-4	garlic cloves, minced (optional)	3-4
	salt and pepper to taste	

PASTRY:

5 cups	flour	1.25 L
1 tbsp.	salt	15 mL
1½ cups	lard	375 mL
1 cup	water, approximately	250 mL

In a large bowl, combine meat, onions, garlic, salt and pepper. Set aside. If the mouth of your baking pot is small, you will need less pastry. Mix together flour and salt. Cut in lard with a pastry blender until mixture resembles coarse meal. Add water, a little at a time, until dough holds together in a ball. Put ⅓ of the meat and onion in a 6-quart (6 L) cast-iron pot. Roll out ⅓ of dough on a floured board to about ¼" (1 cm) thickness. Cut 2 or 3 holes in dough and place it over meat in pot. Spread the rest of the meat evenly over the dough. If you have bones from cut up meat, make a broth and pour beef broth or water to about ¾" (2 cm) from the top. Roll out the rest of the dough and top the second layer of meat. Cut 4 slits on the top crust for steam to escape. You may have to add more water as it bakes. Bake, uncovered, at 350°F (180°C) for 1½ hours, until the top crust is brown. Cover the pot and reduce heat to 275°F (140°C) for 3-3½ hours. This makes a large pie. It is nice with a salad or coleslaw and pickles. I divide the pie and freeze portions of it to reheat later. It's perfect to bring for a crowd when you go skiing. It's even tastier when reheated. You could serve plain boiled potatoes with the pie. I always leave some of the fat on the meat when I am cutting it up, it adds flavor to the pie. **Serves 12-14.**

See photograph on page 123.

STANDING RIB ROAST

This traditional English dinner is a universal favorite.

| 4-5 lb. | rib roast | 1.8-2.2 kg |
| | salt and pepper to taste | |

Place roast in a roasting pan, rib side down. Sprinkle with salt and pepper. Roast at 325°F (160°C) for 1 hour. For medium-rare, reduce heat to 300°F (150°C) or less for 2 hours. Do not cover the roast. If the roast is very lean, ask your butcher for a piece of suet to place on top of the roast while cooking. Use the fat and drippings to make Yorkshire pudding.

See photograph on the front cover.

Yorkshire Pudding

2	eggs	2
1 cup	milk	250 mL
1 cup	flour	250 mL
½ tsp.	salt	2 mL
	beef drippings	

Preheat oven to 400°F (200°C). Pour ½ tsp. (2 mL) of beef fat into each muffin tin. Place muffin tin in oven to heat. Pan and fat should be piping hot before pouring in batter. Beat eggs and milk together; add flour and salt and beat for 2-3 minutes. Fill hot muffin tins ½ full of batter. Bake for 30 to 40 minutes. Serve with roast beef. **Makes 12.**

POT ROAST

This inexpensive cut of meat has a wonderful aroma when cooking and the meat becomes very tender.

4-lb.	chuck roast	1.8 kg
¼ cup	flour	60 mL
4 tbsp.	lard	60 mL
4	large carrots, cut into large pieces	4
8	potatoes, peeled and cut in half	8
2	large onions or 4 small	2
2	garlic cloves, minced	2
2	celery stalks, chopped in large pieces	2
	salt and pepper to taste	
2 cups	beef broth or water	500 mL
1	bay leaf	1

POT ROAST

Continued

Heat lard in roaster on top of the stove. Dredge roast with flour and sear on all sides in roaster. Cover and roast in oven for 1 hour at 375°F (190°C). Prepare vegetables. Place all vegetables around the roast and add salt and pepper to taste. Add beef broth or water and bay leaf. Reduce heat to 300°F (150°C) and roast for 2 hours more. You may have to add a bit more water. Slice meat and arrange on a large platter. Arrange vegetables around the sliced meat. Discard bay leaf. Serve with garlic bread. **Serves 6-8.**

NOTE: I use lard for browning; it browns better than butter or oil.

BEEF & KIDNEY PIE

A good friend introduced me to this favorite English recipe and I have developed my own version.

1 lb.	beef kidney	500 g
1 tsp.	salt	5 mL
1 lb.	sirloin steak, cubed	500 g
3 tbsp.	butter	45 mL
2	onions, chopped	2
1	carrot, cut in chunks	1
2	medium potatoes, cubed	2
2 cups	beef stock	500 mL
	salt & pepper to taste	
	paprika to taste	
½ tsp.	chili powder	2 mL
pinch	savory or basil	pinch
2 tbsp.	flour	30 mL
	pastry for 10" (20 cm) single crust	
	milk	

Soak kidney in salted water for 1 hour. Wash kidney and cut off all fat and membrane. Cut kidney into bite-sized pieces, cover with water and boil for ½ hour. Fry steak cubes in 2 tbsp. (30 mL) butter until no longer pink. Remove steak from pan, add remaining butter and fry kidney. Return steak to the frying pan. Add vegetables, beef stock, salt, pepper, paprika, chili powder and savory or basil. Thicken with flour and pour into a 9" (23 cm) casserole. Cover with pie crust and score 4 holes to allow steam to escape. Brush the crust with milk. Bake for 1½ hours at 350°F (180°C). Use your favorite pie pastry. **Serves 6.**

BEEF TONGUE

2 lbs.	beef tongue	1 kg
	water	
1 tbsp.	salt	15 mL
1	bay leaf	1
1	garlic clove	1

Wash tongue and place in a large pot with enough water to cover. Add salt, bay leaf and garlic clove. Bring to a boil, reduce heat and simmer for 2½ to 3 hours. Remove from liquid and cool. Skin the tongue, cover with plastic wrap and refrigerate. When cold, slice tongue and serve with hot mustard or horseradish. **Serves 4-6.**

SHORT RIBS WITH VEGETABLES

This boiled dinner has a lovely flavor and the meat is very tender.

4 lbs.	beef short ribs	1.8 kg
3	medium onions	3
6	potatoes	6
4	large carrots	4
2	garlic cloves	2
1	whole bay leaf	1
	salt and pepper to taste	

Cut ribs into serving-sized pieces, wash thoroughly and place in a large heavy pot or Dutch oven. Add water to cover, bring to a boil and cook on low heat for 1½ hours. Add vegetables, cut into large pieces, garlic, bay leaf, salt and pepper; simmer for 1 more hour. Be sure there is always broth in the pot. Add water as needed. Serve with Fluffy Horseradish Sauce, page 125 or Horseradish Sauce. **Serves 6.**

Variation: To make a New England boiled dinner, use beef brisket instead of short ribs. Add 1 medium turnip cut into large pieces and 1 small cabbage cut into wedges.

BARBECUED SHORT RIBS

4 lbs.	short ribs	1.8 kg
	salt to taste	
4	garlic cloves	4
1	large onion, sliced, or more	1

BARBECUE SAUCE:

2 cups	barbecue sauce	500 mL
1 cup	ketchup	250 mL
1 cup	brown sugar, or more	250 mL
½ cup	soy sauce	125 mL
1 tbsp.	prepared mustard	15 mL
2 tbsp.	Worcestershire sauce	30 mL
2 tsp.	garlic powder or 2 garlic cloves, minced	10 mL

Cut each rib and put ribs into a pot of water. Boil for 5 minutes. Empty pot into the sink, wash the ribs and return them to the pot. Cover ribs with water. Add salt, garlic and onion. Simmer the ribs slowly for 1½ hours. Remove ribs and put in a roaster or large dish. Combine all sauce ingredients and pour over short ribs. Bake in the oven at 350°F (180°C) for 1 hour. Baste ribs frequently. **Serves 4.**

PAN-FRIED HASH

My husband loved this fricassee. It is easy to make and uses leftovers.

1	large onion, chopped	1
3-4 tbsp.	butter or margarine	45-60 mL
3 cups	chopped roast beef, or more	750 mL
3 cups	diced cooked potatoes, or more	750 mL
	salt and pepper to taste	
2 tbsp.	chopped parsley (optional)	30 mL
1	carrot, grated	1
½ cup	broth, water or leftover gravy	125 mL

In a large frying pan, sauté chopped onion in butter for 2-3 minutes. Add chopped roast beef, potatoes, salt, pepper, parsley, shredded carrot, broth, water or gravy, mix together. Bake hash in a greased 2-quart (2 L) casserole for 30 minutes at 350°F (180°C). If you prefer to heat hash on top of the stove, reduce heat and stir often. **Serves 4.**

VARIATIONS: Try leftover ham or pork instead of roast beef.

PEPPERCORN STEAK

4 x 6-oz.	pieces of sirloin steak	4 x 170 g
4 tbsp.	crushed black peppercorns	60 mL
2 tbsp.	butter or oil	30 mL

RED WINE SAUCE:

1	small onion, finely chopped	1
1/4 cup	cognac (optional)	60 mL
1 cup	red wine	250 mL
1 cup	beef stock	250 mL
1/2 cup	whipping cream	125 mL
1 tbsp.	cornstarch	15 mL
2 tbsp.	cold water	30 mL

Put peppercorns in a plastic bag and pound with a heavy object (mallet or cast-iron pan). Press pepper into both sides of the steaks and fry in butter or oil for 4-5 minutes on each side. Put in oven to keep warm. To make the sauce, combine onion, cognac, wine, beef stock and cream in the pan in which you fried the steaks. Boil for 5-8 minutes to reduce. Thicken sauce with cornstarch mixed with cold water. Ladle over steaks when serving.

NOTE: Don't salt the steak when you fry it in butter. The butter will scorch more quickly. Heat butter until golden, add steak quickly and sear.

CHILI

2 1/2 lbs.	ground beef	1.25 kg
2 cups	chopped onion	500 mL
3	garlic cloves, minced	3
3 tbsp.	chili powder	45 mL
1 tbsp.	sugar	15 mL
1/4 tsp.	crushed red pepper	1 mL
1 1/2 tsp.	dried oregano leaves	7 mL
1 tsp.	dried basil leaves	5 mL
1/4 tsp.	salt	1 mL
1 tsp.	cumin	5 mL
2 x 14 oz.	cans tomatoes	2 x 398 mL
8 oz.	can tomato sauce	250 mL
5 1/2 oz.	can tomato paste	156 mL
3 x 14 oz.	cans kidney beans, drained, or use pork and beans	3 x 398 mL

CHILI

Continued

In a Dutch oven, over medium heat, sauté ground beef. Add chopped onion and garlic. Mix well and cook, stirring, until onions are tender, about 5 minutes. Add all remaining ingredients except beans. Simmer slowly for about an hour. Stir often. Add beans and simmer for 10 more minutes. Serve with fluffy rice. **Serves 8-10.**

NOTE: You can use more beans if you like. I often use pork & beans instead of kidney beans.

DELUXE MEAT LOAF

Mashed potatoes provide a tasty frosting for this special meatloaf.

2	eggs	2
½ cup	milk	125 mL
1½ tsp.	salt	7 mL
1 tsp.	dried thyme leaves or sage	5 mL
¼ tsp.	pepper	1 mL
1 cup	soft bread crumbs	250 mL
2 lbs.	ground beef	1 kg
½ cup	chopped onion	125 mL
2 tbsp.	parsley	30 mL

POTATO TOPPING:

6	medium potatoes, boiled and mashed	6
¼ cup	milk	60 mL
¼ cup	butter or margarine	60 mL
2	egg yolks, beaten	2
1 tsp.	salt	5 mL
	pepper to taste	
dash	cayenne	dash

Beat 2 eggs, add milk, salt, thyme or sage and pepper. Stir in bread crumbs and let soak for 5 minutes. Add ground beef, onion and parsley, and mix well. Pack meat mixture into a greased 5 x 9" (13 x 23 cm) loaf pan. Bake at 350°F (180°C) for 1 hour or more, until done. Boil potatoes, mash, add milk, butter, egg yolks, salt and pepper. Cream until fluffy. Remove meat loaf from pan and place on an ovenproof platter. Spread mashed potatoes on sides and top of meat loaf. Return to oven and brown the potatoes. If you like, sprinkle a bit of cayenne on the mashed potatoes before browning. Serve with a salad. **Serves 6-8.**

VEAL PAPRIKA

This famous Hungarian dish can also be made with chicken. Hungarian paprika is more flavorful than the mild paprika most of us are used to. Try it if you can obtain it.

3 tbsp.	butter or margarine	45 mL
2 lbs.	veal stewing meat in 2"(5 cm) pieces	1 kg
2	onions, chopped	2
1 tsp.	paprika	5 mL
	salt to taste	
1 cup	water	250 mL
8-oz.	pkg. egg noodles	250 g
1 tbsp.	flour	15 mL
1 cup	sour cream	250 mL
	chopped parsley for garnish	

In a Dutch oven, heat butter, add veal and brown. Remove veal pieces as they brown. Reduce heat and add onions and paprika. Fry onions until soft. Return veal to pot, add ³/₄ cup (175 mL) water, cover and heat to boiling and simmer for 1½ hours, until meat is tender. Or you could put the pot in the oven at 300°F (150°C). Add water if necessary. Cook noodles according to directions on package. Drain and keep warm. When meat is tender, mix flour with 2 tbsp. (30 mL) water and thicken stew. Add sour cream and heat but do not boil. Pour veal stew over noodles and garnish with parsley. **Serves 6.**

CURRIED LAMB

2 tbsp.	vegetable oil	30 mL
2 lbs.	boneless lamb, cut into 2" (5 cm) pieces	1 kg
1	apple, peeled and chopped (optional)	1
1 cup	chopped onion	250 mL
2-3 tbsp.	curry powder	30-45 mL
2½ cups	chicken broth	625 mL
½ cup	cold water	125 mL
2 tbsp.	flour	30 mL
½ tsp.	paprika	2 mL
	pepper to taste	
½ tsp.	salt	2 mL

In a Dutch oven, heat oil and brown meat. Remove meat and set aside. In the same pan, sauté apple and onion. Add curry powder, lamb, chicken broth. Simmer for about 1 hour. Mix cold water with flour and stir into lamb mixture. Add paprika, pepper and salt to taste. Serve with fluffy rice or pasta. Always add paprika last. I find that it gets bitter if cooked too long. **Serves 4-6.**

RACK OF LAMB

This delicious Scottish recipe is from my daughter-in-law, Pat.

5-6	racks of lamb (5-6 sides of ribs)	5-6
3	garlic cloves, crushed	3
½ tsp.	crumbled dried rosemary	2 mL
½ tsp.	pepper	2 mL
½ tsp.	dry mustard or 1 tsp. (5 mL) Dijon mustard	2 mL
pinch	salt	pinch
½ cup	vegetable oil	125 mL

Trim fat off lamb and cover the tips of the rib bones, not the meat part, with foil. Crush garlic; add rosemary, pepper, mustard and salt. Add to oil. Rub this over the racks of lamb. Refrigerate for an hour or more. Put racks of lamb in a roasting pan, do not cover. Roast at 350°F (180°C) for about 2 hours. The thermometer should register 160°F (75°C) for rare; 180°F (80°C) for well done. Let rest for 20 minutes before carving. **Serves 5-6.**

ROAST VENISON

Salt pork adds a rich flavor to wild game.

3-4 lb.	venison roast	1.5-2 kg
2-3	garlic cloves, halved	2-3
½ lb.	salt pork, thinly sliced	250 g

Rub the roast all over with garlic. Place venison in a roaster, cover with salt pork slices or tie the salt pork on the roast. Do not cover. Roast for 1½ hours at 375°F (190°C). Reduce heat the last ½ hour. If you like it well-done, roast for ½ hour longer. Do not salt the roast, the salt pork will provide the salt. **Serves 4.**

VARIATION: Substitute moose for venison.

MOOSE STEAK CASSEROLE

2 lbs.	moose steak, about 1" (2.5 cm) thick	1 kg
	lard for frying	
2	garlic cloves, chopped	2
2 tbsp.	cornstarch	30 mL
1 tsp.	salt	5 mL
1 tbsp.	dry mustard	15 mL
¼ tsp.	pepper	1 mL
1	large carrot, diced	1
1	large onion, sliced	1
2	celery stalks, sliced	2
14 oz.	can tomato sauce	398 mL
½ cup	barbecue sauce	125 mL

Cut steak into serving-sized pieces. In a frying pan, heat lard. Combine garlic, cornstarch, salt, mustard and pepper. Dip pieces of moose steak into cornstarch mixture. Fry in hot lard. When steak is browned on both sides put into a 4-quart (4 L) casserole. Put chopped carrots, onion and celery over the steak; pour tomato sauce and barbecue sauce over steak and vegetables. Bake for 2 hours. Start the casserole at 400°F (200°C). After 30 minutes, reduce heat to 275°F (140°C). **Serves 4.**

COUNTRY
FLAVORS

Savory &
Sweet Sauces,
Jams,
Pickles
& Relishes

MEDIUM WHITE SAUCE

With this basic you can make mushroom sauce, celery sauce, cheese sauce, etc.

2 tbsp.	butter or margarine	30 mL
2 tbsp.	flour	30 mL
½ tsp.	salt	2 mL
dash	pepper	dash
1 cup	milk	250 mL

In a saucepan, melt butter; stir in flour, salt and pepper. Add cold milk and stir while cooking, until it thickens. **Makes 1 cup (250 mL).**

VARIATIONS: For Cheese Sauce, add ¾ cup (175 mL) cheese, more or less to taste. Stir until cheese is melted. Serve with vegetables. Try any of your favorite cheeses, e.g., blue, Cheddar, Swiss, etc.

CREAMY MUSHROOM SAUCE

In recipes that call for cream of mushroom soup, this makes a wonderful substitute.

2-3 cups	sliced or finely chopped mushrooms	500-750 mL
3 tbsp.	butter or margarine	45 mL
1 tbsp.	flour	15 mL
1 cup	whipping cream	250 mL
½ tsp.	pepper	2 mL

In a frying pan, heat butter, sauté mushrooms until soft; sprinkle with flour; add whipping cream and pepper. Simmer gently for 2 or 3 minutes. **Makes about 2 cups (500 mL).**

VARIATIONS: Instead of all whipping cream, use half sour cream. If you like, add 1 tbsp. (15 mL) chopped dill. For Onion Mushroom Sauce, sauté 1 cup (250 mL) chopped onions with mushrooms, proceed as above.

FRENCH SPECIALTIES

Cipâte, page 111
Spinach Salad, page 60
French Bread, page 31
Chicken Liver Pâté, page 43
Mustard Pickles, page 136
Sugar Pie, page 153

HOLLANDAISE SAUCE

This rich classic sauce is a little tricky to make. Don't be intimidated — it's worth it.

3	egg yolks	3
2 tbsp.	cold water	30 mL
1/2 cup	butter	125 mL
2 tbsp.	lemon juice	30 mL
1/4 tsp.	salt	1 mL
dash	cayenne	dash

It is important to follow the directions carefully. In the top of a double boiler, with a wire whisk, beat egg yolks with cold water until blended. Cook over hot, not boiling, water. Stir constantly with whisk until the mixture begins to thicken, about 1 minute. Add butter, 1 tbsp. (15 mL) at a time. Beat continuously after each addition. Remove from heat and add lemon juice, salt and cayenne. Stir as you add lemon juice. Keep warm over hot water. **Makes 1 cup (250 mL).**

GARLIC SAUCE

Versatile and delicious, this sauce has French and Spanish influences.

8	garlic cloves, chopped	8
1	egg	1
1 tbsp.	prepared mustard	15 mL
1/2 tsp.	salt	2 mL
	pepper to taste	
1/2 cup	olive oil	125 mL
1	lemon, juice of	1

Put chopped garlic and the rest of the ingredients into a food processor, process until sauce is smooth. This sauce will keep in the refrigerator for a week. Use for ribs, fish or vegetables. Try as a dip for dark rye bread or spread on French bread and toast in the oven. **Makes about 3/4 cup (175 mL).**

FLUFFY HORSERADISH SAUCE

Serve with roast beef, corned beef or beef ribs.

1/2 cup	whipping cream	125 mL
3 tbsp.	horseradish	45 mL
1/8 tsp.	salt	0.5 mL

Whip cream until soft peaks form. Fold in horseradish and salt. **Makes about 1 cup (250 mL).**

HORSERADISH SAUCE

This makes a tangy dip for tiny meatballs.

4 oz.	cream cheese	115 g
1/2 cup	sour cream	125 mL
1-2 tbsp.	prepared horseradish	15-30 mL
1 tbsp.	prepared mustard	15 mL

Mix all ingredients together. Put in a small jar and keep in refrigerator. Allow the sauce to set for a day. **Makes 1 cup (250 mL).**

VARIATION: For appetizers, add dry mustard if you want a hotter sauce.

HOT HORSERADISH MUSTARD

This is very good with roast beef or ham.

1/2 cup	dry mustard	125 mL
3/4 cup	brown sugar	175 mL
1/4 cup	vegetable oil	60 mL
3 tbsp.	prepared horseradish	45 mL
1/3 cup	vinegar	75 mL

Mix all ingredients together until well-blended and sugar is dissolved. Put in small jars and refrigerate. **Makes about 2 cups (500 mL).**

Variation: If you like the mustard hot, add 1 or 2 more tsp. (5-10 mL) of dry mustard.

TANGY MUSTARD SAUCE

This sauce goes well with corned beef or pork. Add more mustard if you like it hotter.

1/4 cup	butter	60 mL
1/4 cup	flour	60 mL
1/4 cup	dry mustard	60 mL
3 tbsp.	sugar	45 mL
2 tsp.	salt	10 mL
1/2 tsp.	cayenne	2 mL
2 cups	milk	500 mL
2	eggs, beaten	2
1/2 cup	vinegar	125 mL

In a saucepan, melt butter, stir in flour, mustard, sugar, salt and cayenne. Stir in cold milk; heat and stir until thick. Add beaten eggs and bring to a boil for 1-2 minutes. Stir in vinegar. Pour into sterilized jars. Store in refrigerator. **Makes about 1 quart (1 L).**

HOT GARLIC MUSTARD

This spicy garlic sauce is good with any meat, on vegetables or on Italian bread.

1½ cups	white wine	375 mL
1	large onion, finely chopped	1
3	garlic cloves, minced	3
4 oz.	can dry mustard	115 g
2 tbsp.	honey	30 mL
2 tbsp.	vegetable oil	30 mL
1 tsp.	salt	5 mL
3 drops	hot pepper sauce	3 drops
¼ tsp.	turmeric	1 mL

In an enameled or stainless steel saucepan, combine wine, onion and garlic. Boil for 5 minutes. Let cool. Strain. Put strained mixture in saucepan. Add remaining ingredients, boil until thickened. Pour into small jars and let stand 2-3 days before using. **Makes about 2 cups (500 mL).**

LITTLE ACRES BAR-B-Q SAUCE

When my son, Ray, operated Little Acres Bar-B-Q, we used to make 30-40 gallons of this sauce at a time. It is good for ribs, chicken or steak.

2 cups	barbecue sauce, your favorite brand	500 mL
1 cup	ketchup	250 mL
¼ cup	Worcestershire sauce	60 mL
¼ cup	vinegar	60 mL
1 cup	brown sugar	250 mL
½ cup	vegetable oil	125 mL
2 tbsp.	prepared mustard	30 mL
½ cup	soy sauce	125 mL
4	garlic cloves, minced	4
1 tsp.	salt	5 mL
½ tsp.	pepper	2 mL

Mix all ingredients well and refrigerate. If you like your sauce sweeter, add more sugar. This sauce keeps forever in the refrigerator. **Makes about 5 cups (1.25 L).**

Variations: Try white sugar or maple syrup instead of brown sugar.

RED WINE STEAK SAUCE

Use as a French dip for dipping steak and rolls or serve with steak, meat loaf or hamburger patties.

½	small onion, finely chopped	½
1 cup	butter	250 mL
1 tbsp.	parsley	15 mL
¼ cup	red wine	60 mL
2 tbsp.	red wine vinegar	30 mL
1 tsp.	tomato paste or 1 tomato, chopped	5 mL
2	egg yolks, beaten	2

Sauté onion in butter, add remaining ingredients, except yolks, and cook for 3 minutes. Add some of the hot sauce to beaten egg yolks and then add yolks to thicken sauce. Stir in carefully so sauce doesn't curdle. Just bring to a boil and serve. **Makes about 2 cups (500 mL).**

TERIYAKI MARINADE

This garlicky marinade is good with steak, chicken or shrimp.

¼ cup	cooking oil	60 mL
¼ cup	soy sauce or teriyaki sauce	60 mL
¼ cup	dry sherry	60 mL
1 tsp.	ground ginger	5 mL
2	garlic cloves, minced	2
4 tbsp.	brown sugar	60 mL
1 tbsp.	Worcestershire sauce	15 mL

Combine all ingredients. To marinate meat, place meat in a plastic bag; pour marinade in bag and place bag in a bowl. Marinate for 6 hours or overnight in refrigerator. Keep the marinade to baste meat during the last few minutes of cooking. **Makes enough marinade for 2 lbs. (1 kg) of meat.**

CRANBERRY AND RAISIN SAUCE

This is a lovely sauce to serve with ham, turkey, chicken, goose or duck.

1½ cups	sugar	375 mL
1 cup	water	250 mL
4 cups	whole cranberries, fresh or frozen	1 L
½-¾ cup	raisins, well-washed	125-175 mL

Combine sugar and water in saucepan. Boil until sugar is dissolved. Add cranberries and raisins to syrup and simmer until cranberries are cooked, about 8 minutes. Keeps in refrigerator for 2-3 weeks. You can freeze this sauce. **Makes about 1 quart (1 L).**

APPLESAUCE

Try this sauce with ham, pork, chicken or potato pancakes. It is also great with gingerbread or by itself for a simple dessert.

4	large apples, peeled, cored and coarsely chopped	4
½ cup	water	125 mL
¾ cup	brown or white sugar	175 mL
¼ tsp.	cinnamon	1 mL

Heat apples and water until boiling. Stir in sugar and boil for 8-10 minutes. Add cinnamon and remove from heat. **Makes about 3 cups (750 mL).**

RASPBERRY SAUCE

A delicious sauce for ice cream or cheesecake.

6 cups	raspberries	1.5 L
½ cup	water	125 mL
1 cup	sugar	250 mL
2 tbsp.	cornstarch	30 mL
1 cup	currant or apple jelly	250 mL

Combine raspberries, water and sugar. Boil for 5 minutes. Strain and cool. Stir cornstarch into cold juice and bring to a boil; cook until thick. Remove from heat and stir in jelly. Keeps in refrigerator for 2 weeks. **Makes about 3 cups (750 mL).**

SUCRE À CRÉME

I've made this superb sauce for over 50 years. It is an old French recipe from my husband's family. If you are lucky enough to get real farm cream it is even better.

2 cups	whipping cream	500 mL
3 cups	brown or yellow sugar	750 mL
1 tsp.	vanilla or maple flavoring	5 mL
pinch	salt	pinch

In a heavy pot, combine whipping cream and brown sugar. Bring to a boil. Boil for about 3 minutes, stirring constantly. Remove from heat and add flavoring and salt. Store in a covered jar. This keeps indefinitely in the refrigerator. Serve over ice cream or a piece of plain cake. **Makes about 3 cups (750 mL).**

VARIATION: For Caramel Icing, combine 3 tbsp. (45 mL) Sucre à Créme, 2 tbsp. (30 mL) milk and enough icing sugar to make a smooth icing. Use on chocolate cake, spice cake or plain cake.

NOTE: If the sugar crystallizes, add ½ cup (125 mL) cream and boil again for 2-3 minutes.

See photograph on page 175.

RUM CREAM SAUCE

This sauce is a perfect partner for any steamed pudding, gingerbread or apple cake.

¼ cup	butter	60 mL
1 cup	packed brown sugar	250 mL
½ tsp.	cornstarch	2 mL
3	egg yolks	3
1 cup	creamilk (10% m.f.)	250 mL
2 tbsp.	light or dark rum	30 mL
2	egg whites	2

In the top of a doubler boiler, cream together butter, sugar and cornstarch; add yolks and beat well. Gradually blend in creamilk, stirring well to prevent lumps. Cook over simmering water, stirring constantly, until thickened and smooth; stir in rum. (Sauce can be prepared to this point, covered and refrigerated. Reheat gently before continuing with recipe.) In large bowl, beat egg whites until glossy peaks form; stir about ¼ of the egg whites into the cream sauce, then fold sauce into egg whites. **Makes about 2½ cups (625 mL).**

BROWN SUGAR SAUCE

Use this lovely caramel sauce on puddings, fruit and cakes.

1 cup	brown sugar	250 mL
2 tbsp.	cornstarch	30 mL
¼ tsp.	salt	1 mL
2 tbsp.	cold water	30 mL
2 cups	boiling water	500 mL
2 tsp.	lemon juice	10 mL
1 tsp.	vanilla	5 mL
1 tbsp.	butter	15 mL

In a heavy saucepan, combine brown sugar with cornstarch and salt. Mix with cold water. Add boiling water and lemon juice; stir while cooking. Add vanilla and butter and boil for a minute or 2. This sauce keeps well in the refrigerator. **Makes about 2 cups (500 mL).**

FOUR FRUIT MARMALADE

This combination of flavors is superb. This makes a very good gift for Christmas or anytime.

1	large and 2 small oranges (I use Sunkist with no seeds)	1
2	limes	2
1	grapefruit (choose grapefruit that has thin skin)	1
1	large lemon	1
3 cups	water	750 mL
8-9 cups	sugar, do not use less	2-2.5 L

Wash all fruit, trim ends. Cut fruit in half. Lay flat side on board and with a very sharp knife slice fruit as thinly as you can. When all fruit is prepared, put it into a heavy enamel or stainless steel kettle. Add water and bring to a boil. Reduce heat and simmer for at least 50 minutes. Stir while it simmers. Add sugar a cup (250 mL) at a time and stir until sugar is completely dissolved. When marmalade comes to a boil, simmer over low heat for about 30-40 minutes. After you add the sugar, stir marmalade often to be sure it doesn't scorch. Take a spoonful of marmalade and put on a plate. Put plate in refrigerator to cool for 5 minutes or so. If marmalade jells, ladle it into hot sterilized jars and seal. If it does not jell, continue to cook for 10-15 minutes. **Makes 2 quarts (2 L).**

APRICOT JAM

1 lb.	dried apricots	500 g
	water	
19 oz.	can crushed pineapple	540 mL
4 lbs.	sugar	1.90 kg
2	lemons, juice of	2

Place apricots in a heavy pot. Barely cover with water. Let stand overnight. Bring to a boil and simmer, in the same water, until soft. Add pineapple and sugar. Using a potato masher, mash the apricot mixture; stir in the lemon juice. Cook on low heat for 1 hour. Pour into sterilized jars and seal. **Makes about 3 quarts (3 L).**

NOTE: Always boil the rubber rings or sealer lids for 2-3 minutes before sealing your jars.

COMPÔTE

How many of us remember having dried fruit as dessert? Sixty years ago I don't remember having fresh fruit. Apples some times, only in the fall. Oranges at Christmas. But the little general store always carried dried fruit. Mom never used oranges or lemons when she made compôte. I have added a slice or two of orange or lemon.

2 lbs.	dried mixed fruit	1 kg
½ cup	raisins	125 mL
	water	
1 cup	sugar	250 mL
2	orange slices	2
2	lemon slices	2

In a large enamel pot, combine dried fruit and raisins and cover with water. Let fruit soak for 2-3 hours. Bring to a boil over medium heat; stir in sugar. Simmer until fruit is tender, about 1 hour. Add more water if necessary. During the last 10 minutes, add the orange and lemon slices. Cool mixture then remove fruit and place in a glass jar. Cover and refrigerate. Keeps for 2 weeks. Recipe may be halved. **Makes about 2 quarts (2 L).**

NOTE: This recipe may be halved.

GINGERED PEACH CHUTNEY

Try this with chicken, pork or shrimp.

10	ripe peaches, peeled, pitted and cut into small pieces, about 4 cups (1 L)	10
2	lemons, grated zest of	2
1	lemon, juice of	1
2 cups	white sugar	500 mL
1½ cups	cider vinegar	375 mL
3 tbsp.	finely grated or chopped fresh ginger root	45 mL
½ tsp.	salt	2 mL
1 tsp.	mustard seed	5 mL
1	medium onion, chopped	1
1	garlic clove, minced	1
1 cup	golden raisins	250 mL
⅛ tsp.	cayenne	0.5 mL

In a nonaluminum bowl, toss peaches, lemon zest and juice. Set aside. In a heavy saucepan, combine sugar, vinegar, ginger, salt, mustard seed, onion and garlic. Bring to a boil over medium heat, reduce heat and simmer for 10 minutes. Add peaches, juices and raisins to pan. Return to heat and simmer 45 minutes, until syrup is thick, stirring constantly. Remove from heat, add cayenne and stir. Fill sterilized jars and seal. Store in a cool dark place. **Makes about 2 quarts (2 L).**

HERBED VINEGAR

1 qt.	white wine vinegar	1 L
2-3	sprigs fresh herbs such as rosemary, thyme, basil or oregano.	2-3
2-3	large garlic cloves or shallots	2-3
1	small, fresh or dry, hot green or red pepper	1

In a small nonaluminum pan over medium heat, bring vinegar to a boil. Remove from heat. Place herbs, garlic or shallots and pepper into small bottles or sterilized jars with tightly fitting lids. Ladle warm vinegar through a funnel into bottles and seal. Place in a dark place for a month before serving. Keeps about a year unrefrigerated. **Makes 1 quart (1 L).**

VARIATIONS: For Pepper Vinegar use dried whole red peppers instead of herbs. Chive blossoms and stems look very decorative in tall bottles and add a subtle onion flavor.

PICKLED CRAB APPLES

These add color to a cold meat platter and are very tasty with turkey, pork chops or roast pork.

7 lbs.	crab apples	3 kg
1 qt.	cider vinegar	1 L
3 cups	white sugar, or more if desired	750 mL
3	sticks whole cinnamon	3
2 tbsp.	whole cloves	30 mL
1 tsp.	whole allspice	5 mL

Wash crab apples. Leave stem but remove the blossom end. In an enamel or stainless steel kettle, combine remaining ingredients and bring to a boil. Add crab apples to the syrup and boil about 5 minutes. Remove from heat, cover and let stand overnight. Pack crab apples into sterilized jars. Strain syrup, boil and pour over crab apples and seal. Crab apples are ready to use after 2-3 weeks. **Makes about 5 quarts (5 L).**

PICKLED EGGS

Pickled eggs are a great snack or appetizer and go well with cold meats.

12	eggs	12
	cold water	
1 tbsp.	vinegar	15 mL
1 tbsp.	chopped onion	15 mL
½	red pepper, cut into strips (optional)	½
1 tbsp.	salt	15 mL
3 cups	white vinegar	750 mL
1 cup	water	250 mL
1 tsp.	sugar	5 mL

Cover eggs with cold water and 1 tbsp. (15 mL) vinegar. Boil for 5 minutes. Set aside and let stand in hot water for 30 minutes. Peel eggs and place in jars. Boil remaining ingredients for 7-8 minutes and pour over eggs. Seal; refrigerate and let stand for a few days before using. **Makes 1 dozen.**

VARIATION: Add 1 tbsp. (15 mL) pickling spice, 5 or 6 whole cloves, 1 garlic clove, 1 or 2 pieces of ginger root and 1 finely sliced onion.

DILLED CARROTS

Serve these crisp pickles with sandwiches or cold meat and salads.

	fresh dill	
	garlic (3-4 cloves per jar)	
6 qts.	crisp raw carrots	6 L
10 cups	water	2.5 L
3 cups	vinegar	750 mL
¾ cup	pickling salt	175 mL
½ cup	sugar	125 mL

Sterilize jars. Place 2 sprigs of fresh dill with seeds and 3-4 cloves of garlic in each jar. Clean carrots and cut into carrot sticks as long as can fit into jars. Baby carrots may be left whole. Fill jars with carrot sticks. In a large saucepan, combine water, vinegar, salt and sugar, boil for 7-8 minutes. Pour boiling mixture over carrots and seal. Let carrots mature for 3-4 weeks. **Makes about 6 quarts (6 L).**

VARIATION: For Dilled Cauliflower, substitute cauliflower florets for carrots.

See photograph on page 51.

MILLION DOLLAR PICKLES

4 qts.	sliced unpeeled cucumbers	4 L
8-10	medium-sized onions, sliced	8-10
¾ cup	coarse pickling salt	175 mL
1	each, red and green pepper, seeded and sliced in strips (optional)	1
1 qt.	white vinegar	1 L
4 cups	white sugar	1 L
1 tsp.	celery seed	5 mL
1 tsp.	turmeric	5 mL
2 tbsp.	mustard seed	30 mL
1 tbsp.	pickling spices	15 mL

Use cucumbers that are not too big. Prepare the cucumbers and onions and place in a stainless steel bowl or crock. Sprinkle with salt and add enough water to just cover the vegetables. Let stand for 2-3 hours. Drain and rinse with cold water. In a 3-gallon (12 L) enamel pot, combine vinegar, sugar and the spices tied in a bag. Let mixture come to a boil. Add the drained vegetables and peppers and just let this come to a boil. Do not boil more than 2 or 3 minutes. Pack into hot sterilized jars. Let stand for 2 or 3 weeks before using. **Makes about 8 quarts (8 L).**

See photograph on page 51.

MUSTARD PICKLES

Once you've tasted these, you'll never buy mustard pickles again. They make very good gifts. I give away at least 60 jars every year.

1	medium-sized head of cauliflower, cut into small pieces	1
3 qts.	cucumbers, chopped into small cubes	3 L
4	large onions, chopped or 2 lbs. (1 kg) pickling onions	4
8	small green tomatoes, cut into pieces	8
4 qts.	water	4 L
1 cup	pickling salt	250 mL
3 cups	string beans, cut into very small pieces	750 mL
2	red peppers, seeded and finely chopped	2
2	green peppers, seeded and finely chopped	2

MUSTARD SAUCE:

6 cups	vinegar	1.5 L
½ cup	dry mustard	125 mL
1½ tsp.	turmeric	7 mL
5-6 cups	light brown or white sugar	1.25-1.5 L
1 cup	flour	250 mL
1 tsp.	celery seed	5 mL

Put cauliflower, cucumbers, onion and green tomatoes in a glass or stainless steel bowl or small crock. In a large pot, bring 4-quarts (4 L) water to a boil; add pickling salt. Pour hot brine over the cauliflower mixture and let sit overnight. Next morning, drain and wash the vegetables in cold water; just a good rinse. Put vegetables aside. Boil beans in unsalted water for 10 minutes. Drain and add to cauliflower mixture. Put vinegar in a stainless steel pot. In a bowl, combine mustard, turmeric, sugar and flour. Add a little of the cold vinegar and mix to a thin paste. Add mustard paste to vinegar and stir constantly while it cooks and thickens. Add celery seed. When mustard sauce comes to a boil, add vegetables, except peppers. Stir while cooking, just until the vegetables come to a boil. Add peppers and boil for 1-2 minutes. Put into sterilized sealers. You can vary the vegetables, or use less of 1 and more of the other. Yellow or green beans or both are good. **Makes 6-7 quarts (6-7 L).**

See photograph on page 123.

NOTE: Do not cook vegetables too long. They should be crisp.

DILL PICKLES

These are the Ukrainian pickles that my mother used to make. Add ½ cup (125 mL) sugar if you want to enhance the flavor.

2	sprigs of fresh dill per jar	2
10 lbs.	pickling cucumbers, scrubbed	4.5 kg
1 tsp.	pickling spices per jar	5 mL
2-3	garlic cloves per jar	2-3
20 cups	water	5 L
1 cup	pickling salt	250 mL
2 cups	vinegar	500 mL

Place dill in bottom of clean jars. Add cucumbers, spices and garlic. Bring the water, salt and vinegar to a boil. Pour boiling mixture over the cucumbers and seal. Always put rubber rings or tops into boiling water for a minute or 2 before you use them. **Makes about 10-12 quarts (10-12 L).**

SPICED PICKLED BEETS

4 qts.	beets	4 L
4 cups	vinegar	1 L
3 cups	white sugar	750 mL
1 cup	water	250 mL
1 tbsp.	salt	15 mL
1 tsp.	allspice	5 mL
2 tbsp.	whole cloves tied in cheesecloth	30 mL

Select small young beets, scrub clean, leave root and about 2" (5 cm) of stem. Boil beets for 1 hour, or just until tender. Put cooked beets in the sink and rinse with cold water. With a knife, cut off root and stem. Rub beets under cold water and skin will slip off. Have sterilized jars ready. Cut beets into desired thickness and pack in jars. Boil remaining ingredients together for 7-8 minutes, and pour over the beets. Seal jars. **Makes 4 quarts (4 L).**

HOT & SWEET PEPPER RELISH

6	red bell peppers, seeded and chopped	6
6	green bell peppers, seeded and chopped	6
2	jalapeño or 3 serrano chili peppers, seeded and chopped	2
4	medium onions, chopped	4
	boiling water	
1 cup	cider vinegar	250 mL
1½ cups	sugar	375 mL
4 tsp.	salt	20 mL
2 tsp.	celery seed	10 mL
2 tsp.	mustard seed	10 mL

Place chopped peppers and onions into a large heavy saucepan. Add boiling water to cover. Let stand 5 minutes, drain well. Wash and dry saucepan. While peppers drain, bring vinegar, sugar, salt, celery seed and mustard seed to a boil in the same saucepan over medium heat. Boil 5 minutes; add drained peppers and onions; lower heat and simmer 10 minutes, or until vegetables are tender but still crisp. Pack relish into sterilized jars; leave ½" (1 cm) space at the top of each jar. Seal. Store in a cool dark place at least 3 weeks before using. **Makes 1½ quarts (1.5 L).**

BRINE FOR SOUR CABBAGE HEAD

12 qts.	boiling water	12 L
2 cups	pickling salt	500 mL
	whole cabbages, trimmed and cored	

Boil water and salt together and cool. Place cabbage in a crock. Pour brine over cabbage heads. Place a large plate on the cabbage and place a heavy weight on the plate so the brine is at least 3" (7 cm) over the cabbage. Keep in warm place for three weeks. When the cabbage is sour, remove from the crock and place cabbage leaves or heads in plastic pails and freeze until ready to use.

COUNTRY
FLAVORS

Desserts, Pies, Cakes, Squares, Cookies & Candies

MAPLE SYRUP BANANAS

A simple, quick recipe — try apples instead of oranges.

½ cup	maple syrup	125 mL
½ cup	brown sugar	125 mL
4 tbsp.	lemon juice	60 mL
2 tbsp.	butter	30 mL
4	bananas, peeled and halved lengthwise	4
1	large orange, sectioned, sections halved	1
½ cup	whole pecans	125 mL

In a heavy frying pan, over low heat, combine syrup, sugar, lemon juice and butter; bring to a boil. Gently lay the bananas, orange pieces and pecans in hot syrup. Stir gently and baste the bananas. Serve over plain ice cream or top with whipped cream. **Serves 4.**

BAKED BANANAS

¼ cup	butter or margarine	60 mL
3	bananas	3
½ cup	brown sugar	125 mL
2 tbsp.	lemon juice	30 mL
¼ tsp.	allspice	1 mL
½ cup	light rum	125 mL
	whipped cream	

Heat oven to 350°F (180°C). Melt butter in an 8" (20 cm) baking dish. Split bananas in half lengthwise and lay them in the dish. Mix brown sugar, lemon juice and allspice. Sprinkle over bananas. Bake, uncovered, for 15-20 minutes. Turn bananas often to coat them with sugar mixture. Pour rum over bananas and bake another 5 minutes just to heat the rum. Serve with whipped cream. **Serves 2-3.**

CHOCOLATE FONDUE

Dip fresh fruit pieces, strawberries, pineapple, apricots, peaches, apples, etc. in this creamy sauce. Also try Pound Cake.

6 tbsp.	whipping cream	90 mL
2 cups	milk or dark chocolate chips	500 mL
⅛ tsp.	cinnamon	0.5 mL
2 tbsp.	brandy	30 mL

Heat cream in a fondue pot. Add chocolate chips; stir to melt and make a smooth sauce. Stir in remaining ingredients. **Serves 4.**

BURNT CRÈME

The crisp caramelized topping is a delicious contrast to this rich creamy custard. Crème Brûlée is a French favorite. The topping can also be made with maple sugar.

2 cups	whipping cream	500 mL
4	egg yolks	4
½ cup	sugar	125 mL
1 tbsp.	vanilla	15 mL
	brown sugar for dusting cups	

Preheat oven to 350°F (180°C). Heat cream to very hot but do not boil. Beat the egg yolks with sugar until light. Beat cream into egg yolks. Stir in vanilla. Pour mixture into 6 individual custard cups. Place cups in a baking dish and pour in 1" (2.5 cm) water. Bake for about 40 minutes. Remove cups from water and cool. When cold, sprinkle each custard cup with 2 tsp. (10 mL) of sugar, about ¼-⅓" (1 cm) layer. Put custard cups on a cookie sheet and place on the top shelf in the oven. Turn on broiler. Watch carefully so the sugar does not burn. It will take 2-3 minutes to carmelize the sugar. **Serves 6.**

BLUEBERRY PUDDING

This cobbler-type pudding has been a favorite across Canada for many, many years.

3 cups	fresh or frozen blueberries	750 mL
¾ cup	sugar	175 mL
2 tbsp.	lemon juice	30 mL
½ cup	water	125 mL
½ cup	sugar	125 mL
4 tbsp.	butter or margarine	60 mL
1	egg	1
1 cup	flour	250 mL
1 tsp.	baking powder	5 mL
½ tsp.	salt	2 mL
½ tsp.	vanilla	2 mL
½ cup	milk	125 mL

Combine berries, sugar, lemon juice and water. Bring to a boil, pour into a 3-quart (3 L) baking dish. Cream sugar and butter, add egg and beat. Stir in dry ingredients and just enough milk to make a smooth batter. Drop by spoonfuls onto the hot blueberry mixture. Bake at 350°F (180°C) for 45-60 minutes. Serve with ice cream, whipping cream or whipped cream. **Serves 6-8.**

See photograph on page 157.

CARAMEL APPLE PUDDING

1 cup	flour	250 mL
1 tsp.	baking powder	5 mL
1 tsp.	cinnamon	5
1/4 tsp.	salt	1 mL
1/2 cup	white or brown sugar	125 mL
2 cups	chopped apples	500 mL
1/2 cup	chopped almonds (optional)	125 mL
1/2 cup	raisins (optional)	125 mL
3/4 cup	milk	175 mL
3/4 cup	brown sugar	175 mL
1/4 cup	butter	60 mL
1 cup	boiling water	250 mL

Sift together flour, baking powder, cinnamon, salt and white sugar. Add chopped apples, almonds and milk. Mix thoroughly. Spread dough in a greased 8 x 10" (20 x 25 cm) baking pan. In another bowl, mix together brown sugar, butter and boiling water until butter melts. Pour over dough. Bake at 350°F (180°C) for 40-50 minutes. Serve warm with ice cream or whipped cream. **Serves 6.**

VARIATION: For Maple Sugar Pudding, use Maple Syrup Sauce instead of Brown Sugar Sauce. Combine 1 1/2 cups (375 mL) maple sugar and 3/4 cup (175 mL) water. Bring to a boil, add 2 tbsp. (30 mL) butter and pour over apple dough, bake as above.

SPICED STEAMED SUET PUDDING

1 cup	finely chopped suet	250 mL
1 cup	fancy molasses	250 mL
1 cup	milk	250 mL
3 cups	flour	750 mL
1/2 tsp.	ginger	2 mL
1/2 tsp.	cloves	2 mL
1/2 tsp.	nutmeg	2 mL
1 tsp.	cinnamon	5 mL
1 tsp.	salt	5 mL
1 tsp.	soda	5 mL
1 cup	raisins, well-washed	250 mL

SPICED STEAMED SUET PUDDING

Continued

In a large bowl, mix suet, molasses and milk. Sift together flour, spices, salt and soda. Add to suet mixture with raisins. Grease a 6-cup (1.5 L) mold or use a 1½ lb. (750 g) coffee can. Fill ⅔ full. In a large pot, place pudding mold and surround with 2" (5 cm) of water. Cover. Just bring to a boil, reduce heat and steam for 3 hours. Serve hot with your favorite sauce or whipped cream. **Serves 8.**

SUET CARROT PUDDING

1 cup	grated raw carrots	250 mL
1 cup	grated potatoes	250 mL
1 cup	chopped suet	250 mL
1¼ cups	brown sugar	300 mL
1½ cups	flour	375 mL
1 tsp.	salt	5 mL
1 tsp.	cinnamon	5 mL
¼ tsp.	cloves	1 mL
¼ tsp.	nutmeg	1 mL
1 tsp.	baking soda	5 mL
1 cup	raisins, well-washed	250 mL
1 cup	currants, well-washed	250 mL

In a large bowl, combine carrots, potatoes, suet and brown sugar. Add the remaining ingredients. Pour mixture into well-greased 1 lb. (500 g) coffee tins. Steam for 3 hours, see above. Remove from tins. Do not keeping pudding in refrigerator, freeze as soon as it is cold. Serve with Rum Sauce, page 130 or Brown Sugar Sauce, page 131. **Serves 12-14.**

NOTE: To cook frozen pudding, steam for 1½ hours.

PINEAPPLE GRAHAM WAFER PUDDING

This light dessert is a family favorite for Christmas dinner.

2	eggs, separated	2
¼ cup	sugar	60 mL
⅓ cup	water	75 mL
1¼ cups	icing sugar	300 mL
½ cup	butter	125 mL
1 tsp.	vanilla	5 mL
pinch	salt	pinch
1½ cups	graham wafer crumbs	375 mL
19 oz.	can pineapple tidbits or chunks, cut into small pieces	540 mL
1½ cups	whipping cream, whipped	375 mL
2-3 tbsp.	icing sugar	30-45 mL

In a small heavy saucepan or double boiler, beat egg yolks, ¼ cup (60 mL) sugar and water. Cook, stirring constantly. Remove pan from heat as soon as the custard is thick and cool. Do not boil this. Cream icing sugar, vanilla, butter and salt until light. Mix custard and icing sugar mixture together. Set aside. Beat 2 egg whites until stiff and carefully fold into the custard mixture. To assemble pudding, place ⅓ of the graham wafer crumbs in a 2-quart (2 L) flat-bottomed glass bowl. Top crumbs with half of the custard then half of the pineapple. Repeat layers with 1/3 of crumbs and remaining custard and pineapple. Top with remaining crumbs, reserving 1 tbsp. (15 mL). Cover pudding with plastic wrap and refrigerate overnight. An hour or 2 before serving, top dessert with whipped cream, sweetened with 2-3 tbsp. (30-45 mL) of icing sugar. You will have a 3-4" (7-10 cm) layer of whipped cream. Top with reserved crumbs. This pudding keeps well for a week or more in the refrigerator. To serve, use a large spoon and dig right to the bottom of the pudding to get all the layers. **Serves 8-10.**

See photograph on the back cover.

BREAD PUDDING — OLD FASHIONED

6	slices of bread , buttered and cut into large pieces	6
½ tsp.	cinnamon	2 mL
½ cup	raisins, well-washed	125 mL
½ cup	walnuts (optional)	125 mL
4	eggs, well-beaten	4
1 cup	milk	250 mL
½ cup	creamilk (10% m.f.)	125 mL
1 tsp.	grated lemon rind	5 mL
⅔ cup	white or yellow sugar	150 mL

Grease a 3-quart (3 L) casserole and lay half of the buttered bread over the bottom. Sprinkle with a bit of cinnamon and half of the raisins and walnuts, if using. Top with the rest of the bread, cinnamon and raisins. Beat eggs, add milk, creamilk, lemon rind and sugar, pour over bread and fruit. Bake at 350°F (180°C) for 1 hour. Serve warm with cream, whipped cream, Rum Cream Sauce, page 130, Brown Sugar Sauce, page 131 or Sucre Á Crème, page 130. **Serves 6-8.**

VARIATION: Use currants instead of raisins.

PIE OR TART PASTRY

Brown sugar gives this pastry a nice golden color.

2 cups	flour	500 mL
1 tsp.	baking powder	5 mL
2 tbsp.	brown sugar	30 mL
¼ tsp.	salt	1 mL
1 cup	shortening	250 mL
½ cup	milk	125 mL
1 tsp.	vanilla	5 mL

Combine dry ingredients, cut in shortening until crumbs are formed. Add milk and vanilla and mix until dough forms a ball. Roll dough out on a lightly floured surface. Cut to desired size. **Makes enough pastry to make 2, 9" (23 cm) double-crust pies.**

Egg Yolk Glaze

1	egg yolk	1
2 tbsp.	water	30 mL

Beat yolk and water together. Use to brush on pies and pastries.

GRAHAM WAFER CRUST

16	graham wafers (1¼ cups [300 mL])	16
⅓ cup	white sugar	75 mL
⅓ cup	melted butter	75 mL
¼ tsp.	cinnamon (optional)	1 mL

Put wafers in a plastic bag and roll with a rolling pin roll until the crumbs are fine. Or use a food processor. Add sugar and melted butter. Turn the crumb mixture into a 9" (22 cm) pie plate. With the back of a spoon, spread and press crumb mixture on bottom and sides of plate. Bake in oven at 350°F (180°C) for 10-12 minutes. Cool before adding filling. **Makes 1, 9" (23 cm) crust.**

VARIATION: To make Chocolate Wafer Crust, use the same method but substitute chocolate wafers and omit sugar. Chill crust. Do not bake.

RASPBERRY PIE

1¾ cups	flour	425 mL
½ cup	brown sugar	125 mL
½ cup	ground almonds or pecans	125 mL
⅔ cup	butter	150 mL
1	egg, separated	1
4 cups	fresh raspberries	1 L
½ cup	sugar	125 mL

Combine flour, brown sugar, ground almonds, butter and egg yolk. Work in processor or by hand. Press dough over bottom and about 1" (2.5 cm) up the sides of a 10" (25 cm) springform pan or flan pan. Brush crust with slightly beaten egg white. Bake at 350°F (180°C) for 20 minutes. Arrange raspberries on crust, sprinkle with sugar and bake for another 20 minutes. Serve with sweetened whipped cream or ice cream. **Serves 8.**

VARIATION: For Raspberry & Blueberry Pie, use half blueberries and half raspberries. Also try sliced peaches.

See photograph on page 157.

FRESH FRUIT CUSTARD PIE

	pastry for a 10" (25 cm) pie shell	
1	egg white	1
	fresh fruit, see method	
3	egg yolks	3
1 cup	creamilk (10% m.f.)	250 mL
1 tbsp.	cornstarch	15 mL
1 cup	sugar	250 mL
pinch	salt	pinch
1 tsp.	vanilla	5 mL

Use your favorite pie pastry, brush with slightly beaten egg white. Or use the same pastry as raspberry pie, page 146. Use either a springform pan or 10" (25 cm) pie plate. Bake pastry for 10-15 minutes. Slice fruit into thin wedges and arrange in a circle in partly baked pie crust. Use raspberries, pears, plums, apples, peaches, apricots or half rhubarb and strawberries. Beat together remaining ingredients. Pour over fruit in pie shell. Bake at 350°F (180°C) for 40 minutes. Custard should be set. Serve with whipped cream or ice cream. **Serves 8.**

FRESH FRUIT TARTS

	pastry for tart shells	
	fresh fruit, see method	
½ cup	sugar	125 mL
1 cup	whipping cream	250 mL
3 tbsp.	icing sugar	45 mL
½ cup	sour cream	125 mL
1 tsp.	vanilla	5 mL

Use your favorite pastry. Bake shells at 350°F (180°C) for 20 minutes or until golden in color. Set aside. Use fresh peaches, blueberries, raspberries or strawberries. Mash or process 1 cup (250 mL) of the fruit you are going to use with ½ cup (125 mL) sugar. Set aside. Beat whipping cream add icing sugar and beat until stiff. Add sour cream and vanilla, beat until mixed. Put 1 tsp. (5 mL) of puréed fruit into each tart shell. Top with 1 tbsp. (15 mL) of whipped cream mixture. Top with as much fresh fruit as will fit into the tart shell. **Makes about 6, 3" (7.5 cm) tarts.**

CREAM CHEESE FILLING FOR TARTS

4 oz.	cream cheese, at room temperature	125 g
3 tbsp.	sugar	45 mL
1 tsp.	lemon juice	5 mL
½ cup	whipping cream, whipped stiff	125 mL
	tart shells	
	fresh fruit, see method	
	whipped cream for garnish	

Beat cream cheese with sugar and lemon juice until smooth. Gently fold in whipped cream. Use your favorite pastry and bake tart shells until golden, see method for previous recipe. Cool tart shells. When cold, fill ⅔ with cream cheese filling and top with your favorite fruit such as blueberries, peaches, raspberries or strawberries. Top with whipped cream. **Makes about 2 cups (500 mL) of filling.**

PASTRY CREAM

Use this pastry cream for fruit tarts or pies. Fill your baked tart shells half full. Top with fresh blueberries, strawberries, raspberries, or any fruit you like.

2 cups	milk	500 mL
2 tbsp.	cornstarch	30 mL
4	egg yolks, beaten	4
¾ cup	sugar	175 mL
1 tsp.	vanilla	5 mL
¼ tsp.	salt	1 mL
3 tbsp.	Grand Marnier (optional)	45 mL

In a double boiler or a heavy saucepan, stir a little cold milk into the cornstarch, add the rest of the milk, egg yolks, sugar, vanilla and salt. Stir while cooking. When thick, remove from heat and stir in Grand Marnier. Put in a bowl, cover with plastic wrap and chill while you bake tart shells. This pastry cream can also be used for a fresh fruit pie. Top pie or tarts with whipped cream. **Makes about 3 cups (750 mL) of filling.**

APPLE CREAM PIE

	pastry for a 9" (23 cm) double-crust pie	
6 cups	peeled, sliced apples (MacIntosh are good)	1.5 L
1 cup	sugar	250 mL
½ tsp.	cinnamon	2 mL
½ cup	raisins, washed	125 mL
2 tbsp.	butter or margarine	30 mL
	milk	
	sugar	
½ cup	whipping cream	125 mL

Line pie plate with pastry. Mix together apples, sugar, cinnamon and raisins. Put into pie shell. Dot with butter or margarine. Cover with top crust. Cut 2" (5 cm) slits in center of top crust. Brush crust with milk and sprinkle with sugar. Bake at 375°F (190°C) for 50-60 minutes. Ten minutes before the pie is done, pour whipping cream through slits. Finish baking. Serve hot or cold. **Serves 6-8.**

Variation: For Peach Pie, use 6 cups (1.5 L) of sliced, peeled peaches and omit raisins.

PEACH CRUMB PIE

1 cup	brown sugar	250 mL
½ tsp.	cinnamon	2 mL
½ cup	flour	125 mL
¼ tsp.	salt	1 mL
½ cup	chopped pecans or walnuts	125 mL
¼ cup	butter	60 mL
	pastry for a 9" (23 cm) pie shell	
2 cups	sliced peaches	500 mL

Combine sugar, cinnamon, flour, salt and pecans. Add butter and mix. Put half the mixture into the pie shell. Cover with sliced peaches and top with remaining crumbs. Bake at 350°F (180°C) for 30-40 minutes. Serve topped with whipped cream or ice cream. **Serves 6-8.**

FRESH PLUM LATTICE PIE

10	fresh plums, or more	10
1½ cups	sugar	375 mL
¼ cup	cornstarch	60 mL
½ tsp.	ground ginger	2 mL
½ tsp.	salt	2 mL
1 tbsp.	butter	15 mL
1 tsp.	grated orange zest	5 mL
1 tbsp.	orange juice	15 mL
	pastry for a 9" (23 cm) double-crust pie	

Quarter, pit and measure plums to get 1 quart (1 L). In a large saucepan, combine plums, sugar, cornstarch, ginger, salt, butter, orange zest and juice. Heat, stirring, until sugar dissolves, about 10 minutes. Set aside to cool slightly while preparing pastry. Roll out generous half of pastry on lightly floured surface; line a 9" (23 cm) deep-dish pie plate. Roll out remaining pastry on lightly floured surface and cut into strips for lattice top. Pour plum mixture into pastry-lined pie plate. Place strips in lattice pattern on top of pie. Crimp and seal edges. Bake in 425°F (180°C) oven for 10 minutes; reduce temperature to 350°F (180°C) and continue baking 40 minutes more. Cool before serving. **Serves 6-8.**

RHUBARB PIE

1¼ cups	sugar	300 mL
⅓ cup	flour	75 mL
dash	salt	dash
4 cups	rhubarb cut in ½" (1.3 cm) pieces	1 L
	pastry for a 9" (23 cm) double-crust pie	
2 tbsp.	butter	30 mL

Stir together sugar, flour and salt. Add mixture to rhubarb pieces and toss to coat fruit. Fill pastry-lined pie plate with rhubarb, dot with butter. Bake at 375°F (190°C) for 40-50 minutes, until golden brown. **Serves 6-8.**

COCONUT CREAM PIE

	9" (23 cm) baked pie shell	
¾ cup	sugar	175 mL
½ tsp.	salt	2 mL
3 tbsp.	cornstarch	45 mL
3 cups	whole milk	750 mL
3	egg yolks, beaten	3
1 tsp.	vanilla	5 mL
1 cup	toasted Angel Flake coconut	250 mL
	whipped cream	

Prepare your favorite pastry or graham wafer crust. In double boiler, combine sugar, salt and cornstarch. Beat together milk and egg yolks. Stir into dry ingredients. Cook, stirring, until thickened. Remove from heat and stir in vanilla. Put ½ cup (125 mL) toasted coconut in the filling before it's cold. Top pie with whipped cream and sprinkle ½ cup (125 mL) toasted coconut on top of whipped cream. **Serves 6-8.**

LEMON CHIFFON PIE

	9" (23 cm) Graham Wafer Crust, page 146	
1 tbsp.	gelatin (1 env.)	15 mL
¼ cup	water	60 mL
6 tbsp.	sugar	90 mL
3	eggs, separated	3
½ cup	lemon juice	125 mL
½ cup	light syrup	125 mL
1 tsp.	grated lemon rind	5 mL
	whipped cream	
	very thin lemon slices	

In a saucepan, combine gelatin, water and 3 tbsp. (45 mL) sugar. Beat in egg yolks and lemon juice. Stir over low heat or in double boiler until gelatin is dissolved. Stir in syrup and lemon rind. Remove from heat and pour into a large bowl. Cool. In another bowl, beat egg whites until soft peaks form. Add the remaining sugar and beat until stiff. Fold into cold gelatin mixture. Pour into graham crust; chill until firm. Decorate with whipped cream and lemon slices. **Serves 6-8.**

VARIATION: If you like lime pie, substitute lime juice and rind for lemon.

LEMON BUTTER TARTS

3	eggs	3
4 tbsp.	butter	60 mL
1 cup	white sugar	250 mL
2	lemons, juice of	2
12	2" (5 cm) baked tart shells	12
	whipped cream	
	grated lemon rind (optional)	

In double boiler, beat eggs, butter and sugar. Add lemon juice. Continue beating while mixture is cooking. When the mixture is light and thick, remove from stove and put in a bowl. Cover with plastic wrap and refrigerate until cool. Fill small baked shells with lemon butter. Top with whipped cream. If you like lemon rind, sprinkle some on the whipped cream. **Makes 12, 2" (5 cm) tarts.**

See photograph on page 157.

BUTTERSCOTCH PIE

2 cups	milk	500 mL
4 tbsp.	cornstarch	60 mL
	water	
1½ cups	brown sugar	375 mL
3	eggs, separated	3
2 tbsp.	butter	30 mL
1 tsp.	vanilla	5 mL
¼ tsp.	salt	1 mL
	9" (23 cm) baked pie shell	
2 tbsp.	brown sugar	30 mL

Put milk in heavy pot or double boiler. Bring to boiling point and stir in cornstarch mixed with a little water. When thick, add the brown sugar. Beat the egg yolks and add a bit of the hot milk mixture to the egg yolks. Stir the yolks into the milk mixture. Add butter, vanilla and salt. Boil for 2-3 minutes. Fill baked pie shell. Top with meringue made from egg whites beaten until stiff with 2 tbsp. (30 mL) brown sugar. Put in oven to brown at 400°F (200°C) for 10 minutes. Or cover pie with plastic wrap and refrigerate until cool. Top with whipped cream. **Serves 6-8.**

NOTE: You will notice that you thicken the milk before you add the brown sugar. That is to prevent the milk from curdling.

SOUR CREAM RAISIN PIE

2	eggs	2
1 cup	sour cream	250 mL
1 cup	sugar	250 mL
1 cup	raisins, washed	250 mL
1 tbsp.	vinegar	15 mL
1/2 tsp.	cinnamon	2 mL
1/4 tsp.	nutmeg	1 mL
1/4 tsp.	cloves	1 mL
1/2 tsp.	salt	2 mL
	pastry for a 9" (23 cm) single-crust pie	

Beat eggs, add sour cream and sugar and beat until well mixed. Add the rest of the ingredients and pour into pie crust. Bake at 350°F (180°C) for 30-35 minutes, or until a toothpick inserted in center comes out clean. **Makes 1, 9" (23 cm) pie.**

SUGAR PIE

A French Canadian tradition. This pie has many variations. It is just delicious! Don't let the amount of sugar stop you from making this pie. Serve with whipped cream.

	pastry for a 9" (23 cm) single-crust pie	
3	eggs, well-beaten	3
1 cup	brown sugar	250 mL
3/4 cup	white sugar	175 mL
1 1/2 cups	creamilk (10% m.f.)	375 mL
1 tsp.	vanilla	5 mL
1/4 tsp.	salt	1 mL
1 tbsp.	flour	15 mL
	whipped cream for garnish	

Prepare pastry. In a bowl, beat eggs and sugars, add creamilk and beat well. Add vanilla, salt and flour. Pour into unbaked pastry shell. Bake at 325°F (160°C) for 40-50 minutes, or until a knife inserted in center of pie comes out clean. Watch carefully that it doesn't burn. Cool pie. **Serves 6.**

NOTE: If serving the pie with whipped cream, just add half the amount of sugar usually used when you sweeten the cream.

See photograph on page 123.

BUTTER TARTS

These wonderfully delicious Canadian tarts may have been adapted from Sugar Pie, Pecan Pie or old-fashioned vinegar pie.

2 cups	raisins or 1 cup (250 mL) each raisins and currants	500 mL
2	eggs	2
2 cups	brown sugar	500 mL
½ cup	melted butter	125 mL
½ tsp.	salt	2 mL
1 tsp.	vanilla	5 mL
2 tbsp.	vinegar	30 mL
24	unbaked tart shells	24

Soak raisins in hot water and wash well. Beat eggs, add brown sugar, butter, salt, vanilla and vinegar. Beat well. Stir in raisins. Fill tart shells ½ full. Bake for 25 minutes or more at 350°F (180°C). **Makes 24 tarts.**

VARIATION: Add 1 cup (250 mL) chopped pecans, omitting 1 cup (250 mL) raisins.

See photograph on the back cover.

PECAN TARTS

2	eggs	2
½ cup	brown sugar	125 mL
½ cup	corn syrup	125 mL
2 tbsp.	rum (optional)	30 mL
1 tbsp.	flour	15 mL
½ tsp.	salt	2 mL
1 tsp.	vanilla	5 mL
3 tbsp.	melted butter	45 mL
1 cup	pecan halves	250 mL
24	unbaked tart shells	24

In a bowl, beat together eggs, sugar, syrup, rum, flour, salt and vanilla. Stir in butter and pecans. Fill tart shells ⅔ full. Bake at 350°F (180°C) for 30 minutes. To serve, add a dab of whipped cream if you like. **Makes 24 tart shells.**

MINCEMEAT TARTS

1	large apple	1
½ cup	currants or raisins	125 mL
½ cup	brown sugar	125 mL
2 cups	commercial mincemeat	500 mL
1	egg, beaten	1
2 tbsp.	water	30 mL
24	unbaked tart shells	24
1	egg	1
	water	

Peel apple, chop very finely. Wash raisins or currants. Add apple, raisins and brown sugar to mincemeat. Mix well. Use your favorite pastry to line tart shells. Spoon filling into tart shells until ¾ full. Top with pastry cut outs. Brush with egg wash made from egg beaten with water. Bake at 350°F (180°C) for 25-30 minutes. **Makes 24 tarts.**

PUMPKIN PIE

3	eggs, beaten	3
½ cup	brown sugar	125 mL
½ cup	white sugar	125 mL
2 cups	canned or mashed pumpkin	500 mL
1 tsp.	cinnamon	5 mL
1 tsp.	ginger	5 mL
½ tsp.	salt	2 mL
1½ cups	scalded milk or creamilk (10% m.f.)	375 mL
	pastry for a 9" (23 cm) single-crust pie	
	whipped cream, see below	

Beat eggs and sugars, add pumpkin, spices and salt. Stir in hot scalded milk and pour into unbaked pie shell. Bake for 40 minutes at 350°F (180°C), or until a knife inserted into the center of the pie comes out clean. If not, bake a little longer. Cool and spread whipped cream on pie. **Serves 6-8.**

Whipped Cream

1 cup	whipping cream	250 mL
2 tbsp.	icing sugar	30 mL
½ tsp.	vanilla	2 mL

In a very cold bowl, beat cream. Add icing sugar and vanilla and beat until soft peaks form.

CROQUEMBOUCHE

This will make your reputation — glazed cream puffs (profiteroles) are stacked in a pyramid and surrounded with strands of spun sugar. This sounds like a lot of work, but it isn't. It looks spectacular and tastes wonderful.

CREAM PUFF PASTRY:

¾ cup	butter	175 mL
1 cup	water	250 mL
½ tsp.	salt	2 mL
1½ cups	all-purpose flour	375 mL
6	large eggs	6
1½ cups	sugar for syrup	375 mL
4 tbsp.	water	60 mL
	Pastry Cream, page 148	

In a heavy medium-sized pot, combine butter, water and salt and bring to a boil. Remove from stove and stir in flour. Mix quickly while cooking and stir until it all forms a ball and the sides of pot are clean. Remove from heat and add eggs, 1 at a time, beating hard after each addition. Beat until mixture is smooth. Have 2 ungreased cookie sheets ready. Drop dough from a tbsp. (15 mL); space puffs 3" (7 cm) apart. You should have 2 dozen cream puffs. Bake at 375°F (190°C) for 30-40 minutes. The puffs should be a golden color. Cool puffs on a wire rack.

In a heavy frying pan, mix sugar and 4 tbsp. (60 mL) water. Cook over medium heat. Stir while sugar caramelizes. This takes a few minutes. The syrup should be a golden color. Set aside.

With a sharp knife, cut off the top of the cream puffs. Fill each cream puff with 1 tbsp. (15 mL) of pastry cream and replace tops. Form a 9" (23 cm) circle with puffs. Dip the sides of each cream puff in syrup, so they stay in a circle. For the second layer, dip bottom of puff in syrup and stick on top of first layer, slanting layer inward to make a cone-shaped dome. Do the same with the rest of cream puffs until you have 1 on top. You may not need all of the cream puffs to form the cone. Take a spoon and drizzle syrup on top and sides of puffs, it will look like caramelized strings (spun sugar). When ready to serve, pull puffs apart, using 2 forks, and serve. **Serves 12-14.**

VARIATIONS: Make Cream Puffs and bake as above. Fill puffs with flavored whipped cream, adding puréed or finely chopped fruit if you wish, or pastry cream or chocolate custard. For Chocolate Eclairs, make puffs long and thin and frost with chocolate icing. Serve individually.

Fruit Desserts

CHEESECAKE

1 1/2 cups	graham wafer crumbs	375 mL
1/3 cup	melted butter	75 mL
1/4 cup	white sugar	60 mL
2 x 8oz.	pkgs. cream cheese, at room temperature	2 x 250 g
1/2 cup	white sugar	125 mL
4 tbsp.	flour	60 mL
1/2 tsp.	salt	2 mL
1 tsp.	grated lemon rind	5 mL
1 cup	sour cream	250 mL
1 tsp.	vanilla	5 mL
5	eggs, separated	5
1/3 cup	white sugar	75 mL

Mix together crumbs, butter and 1/4 cup (60 mL) sugar and pat into a 10" (25 cm) springform pan. Bake 10-15 minutes at 325°F (160°C). Beat until light, cream cheese, 1/2 cup (125 mL) sugar, flour, salt, lemon rind, sour cream, vanilla and egg yolks. Beat egg whites until soft peak stage. Beat in 1/3 cup (75 mL) sugar and beat until stiff. Fold into cream cheese mixture. Pour into the pan and bake at 325°F (160°C) for 1 hour 15 minutes, or more. Turn off oven and leave cheesecake in oven for 30 minutes. Cool. Serve with sliced strawberries or top with chocolate topping. **Serves 12-14.**

See photograph on page 175.

Chocolate Topping

4 x 1 oz.	squares semisweet chocolate	4 x 30 g
1 cup	sour cream	250 mL

Melt chocolate and mix in sour cream. Spread over cold cheesecake.

Caramel Topping

1/2 cup	whipping cream	125 mL
2 tbsp.	butter	30 mL
1/4 cup	brown sugar	60 mL
1	egg, beaten	1
1/2 cup	chopped walnuts or pecans	125 mL
1/2 tsp.	salt	2 mL

In a saucepan, combine cream, butter, brown sugar and egg. Cook over low heat, stirring, until thick. Remove from heat and stir in nuts and salt. Cool. When cold, pour over chocolate-topped cheesecake or use on plain cheesecake as topping.

Sour Cream Topping

1 cup	sour cream	250 mL
2 tbsp.	white or brown sugar	30 mL
1 tsp.	vanilla	5 mL
1/2 tsp.	salt	2 mL
1 tbsp.	lemon juice	15 mL
1 tsp.	grated lemon rind	5 mL

Beat all ingredients together. Spread on cheesecake.

ORANGE ALMOND CHEESECAKE

CRUST:

1 1/2 cups	graham wafer crumbs	375 mL
1 cup	ground almonds	250 mL
1/4 cup	sugar	60 mL
1/2 cup	melted butter	125 mL

FILLING:

4	eggs	4
1 cup	sugar	250 mL
1/2 cup	creamilk (10% m.f.)	125 mL
1 1/2 lbs.	cream cheese, at room temperature	750 g
2/3 cup	orange juice	150 mL
1 tsp.	vanilla	5 mL
2 tbsp.	amaretto (optional)	30 mL
1/2 tsp.	salt	2 mL

TOPPING:

1 tbsp.	gelatin (1 env.)	15 mL
1/4 cup	lukewarm water	60 mL
1 cup	whipping cream, whipped	250 mL
2 tbsp.	sugar	30 mL
1/2 tsp.	vanilla	2 mL
	orange slices for garnish	

Combine crust ingredients and put in 10" (25 cm) springform pan. Press with a spoon over sides and bottom. Chill in refrigerator for 30 minutes. Beat eggs and sugar. Beat in cream and cream cheese. Add orange juice, vanilla, amaretto and salt. Beat well and pour over graham wafer crust. Bake at 350°F (180°C) for 1 hour, or until set. Remove from oven and cool overnight. Dissolve gelatin in water and cool. Whip cream, add sugar and vanilla. With rubber spatula, fold gelatin into whipped cream. Spread on cold cheesecake. Let set for 2 hours. Garnish with orange slices. **Serves 10-12.**

ANGEL FOOD CAKE

My angel food cake pan is over 50 years old! When we lived on the farm, the fresh farm eggs made wonderful angel food cakes.

1½ cups	egg whites	375 mL
1 cup+2 tbsp.	sifted cake flour	280 mL
1¼ cups	sifted granulated sugar	300 mL
½ tsp.	salt	2 mL
1¼ tsp.	cream of tartar	6 mL
1 cup	sifted granulated sugar	250 mL
½ tsp.	almond extract	2 mL
1 tsp.	vanilla extract	5 mL

Leave egg whites at room temperature overnight or for 3 hours. Heat oven to 350°F (180°C). Sift flour and ½ cup (125 mL) sugar 3 times. Beat egg whites and salt until foamy. Sprinkle with cream of tartar and beat whites until soft peaks form. Slowly, add the 1 cup (250 mL) of sugar, a few tablespoons at a time until stiff and glossy. With a wire whip or spatula, fold in the flour mixture ¼ at a time; fold in flavorings. Pour the batter into an ungreased 9 or 10" (23 or 25 cm) tube pan. Be sure your pan is well washed and there is no trace of grease. Bake for 50-60 minutes. Invert cake over a bottle or funnel to cool. Remove cooled cake and frost or fill as you wish. **Serves 10-12.**

NOTE: Use a glass or stainless steel bowl for egg whites, not plastic.

See photograph on the back cover.

GOLDEN SPICE CAKE

I always make this moist and delicious cake when I make an Angel Food Cake. It uses up the yolks from the angel food.

14	egg yolks	14
1 cup	sugar	250 mL
½ cup	cake flour	125 mL
½ tsp.	cloves	2 mL
1 tsp.	cinnamon	5 mL
2 tsp.	baking powder	10 mL
½ tsp.	salt	2 mL
1 tsp.	vanilla	5 mL
3	egg whites	3

In a large bowl, beat egg yolks and sugar until light. Sift together the cake flour, cloves, cinnamon, baking powder and salt. Stir into the egg yolk mixture; add vanilla. Beat egg whites until stiff; fold into egg yolk mixture. Pour into an ungreased 10" (25 cm) angel food cake pan. Bake at 350°F (180°C) for 60 minutes. Invert as you would an angel food cake. When cake has cooled, sift icing sugar on top or use your favorite icing. **Serves 10-12.**

See photograph on the back cover.

LEMON OR ORANGE CHIFFON

7	egg yolks	7
1½ cups	sugar	375 mL
½ cup	vegetable oil	125 mL
1	lemon, grated rind of (or orange)	1
1 tbsp.	lemon juice (or orange)	15 mL
¾ cup	water	175 mL
2 cups	flour	500 mL
3 tsp.	baking powder	15 mL
½ tsp.	salt	2 mL
7	egg whites	7
½ tsp.	cream of tartar	2 mL

Beat egg yolks and sugar until light. Add oil, lemon rind, juice and water. Beat until well-mixed. Combine flour, baking powder and salt with egg yolks. Wash and dry beater, then beat the egg whites and cream of tartar until very stiff. Fold the stiffly beaten egg whites into the egg yolk mixture. Pour into an ungreased 10" (25 cm) tube cake pan and bake for 1 hour at 350°F (180°C). Invert pan and cool cake before removing it from pan. Gently pass a knife around inside of the pan to ease the cake out of pan. **Serves 10-12.**

POPPY SEED SOUR CREAM CAKE

This is a wonderful cake. For a special look mix 1-2 tsp. (5-10 mL) of poppy seeds into the frosting.

2 cups	cake flour	500 mL
½ tsp.	salt	2 mL
¼ cup	poppy seeds	60 mL
1 cup	butter or margarine	250 mL
1½ cups	sugar	375 mL
4	large eggs, separated	4
1 tsp.	baking soda	5 mL
1 cup	sour cream	250 mL
1 tsp.	vanilla	5 mL

POPPY SEED SOUR CREAM CAKE

Continued

Cut a piece of waxed paper to fit the bottom of a 10" (25 cm) tube or bundt pan. In a large bowl, combine flour, salt and poppy seeds. In another bowl, combine butter and 1 cup (250 mL) sugar, beat until light. Add egg yolks and beat until well-mixed. Mix in baking soda, sour cream and vanilla alternately with the flour and poppy seeds. Beat egg whites until stiff, mix in the remaining sugar. Fold egg white mixture into the batter. Pour batter into prepared pans. Bake at 350°F (180°C) for 1 hour or longer. Ice with lemon icing. Use Butter Icing, page 172,or icing mixed with lemon juice instead of creamilk. **Serves 10-12.**

See photograph on the back cover.

VARIATION: For Spiced Poppy Seed Cake, combine 2 tsp. (10 mL) cocoa, 1 tsp. (5 mL) cinnamon and ⅓ cup (75 mL) white sugar. Spread half of batter in pan. Sprinkle with cocoa mixture; top with remaining batter. Bake as above.

SPONGE CAKE

This is a very good basic cake recipe. Years ago this was one of the most popular cakes.

4	eggs	4
¼ tsp.	cream of tartar	1 mL
1 cup	sugar	250 mL
1 cup	sifted cake flour	250 mL
¾ tsp.	baking powder	3 mL
¼ tsp.	salt	1 mL
¼ cup	water	60 mL
1 tsp.	vanilla	5 mL
1 tsp.	lemon juice	5 mL
	icing sugar	

Separate eggs. Keep egg whites at room temperature for 1 hour. Beat until frothy. Add cream of tartar; beat while adding ½ cup (125 mL) of sugar, a tablespoon (15 mL) at a time, until stiff peaks form. In another bowl, beat yolks until light. Add the remaining sugar and beat until thick and frothy. Combine flour, baking powder and salt. In a measuring cup, combine water, vanilla and lemon juice. At low speed, blend flour mixture, ⅓ at a time, with the water mixture. Add the yolk mixture. Beat 1 minute. Fold in stiffly beaten egg whites. Pour batter into 2, ungreased 9" (23 cm) layer cake pans. Bake at 350°F (180°C) for 25 minutes. Invert cakes on racks to cool. Put together with your favorite jelly or whipped cream. Dust icing sugar on top of cake. Use this cake for peach or strawberry shortcake. **Serves 8-10.**

JELLY ROLL

This is a very simple and very good recipe. I've made it for at least 50 years.

4	large eggs	4
1 cup	sugar	250 mL
1 cup	flour	250 mL
1/2 tsp.	salt	2 mL
1 tsp.	baking powder	5 mL
1 tsp.	vanilla	5 mL
	raspberry jam	

Beat eggs, add sugar and beat until light. Sift together flour, salt and and baking powder. Fold flour into egg mixture. Add vanilla. Pour batter onto greased and floured cookie sheet. Bake at 350°F (180°C) for 20 minutes. Dip a clean dish towel in water and wring until dry. Turn baked jelly roll out onto the towel. Spread with raspberry or your favorite jam or jelly. Gently take edge of towel and roll up cake. Leave roll covered with the towel for 1/2 hour. Remove towel and wrap jelly roll in waxed paper. This freezes very well. Serve with ice cream or use in a trifle. **Serves 8.**

POUND CAKE

1 cup	butter	250 mL
2 cups	sugar	500 mL
1 tsp.	vanilla	5 mL
4	eggs	4
3 cups	flour	750 mL
1 tsp.	baking soda	5 mL
1 tsp.	salt	5 mL
1 cup	buttermilk	250 mL
	powdered sugar	

Beat butter and sugar until fluffy. Beat in vanilla; add eggs, 1 at a time. Mix together flour, soda and salt and add to butter mixture alternately with buttermilk. Pour batter into buttered 10" (25 cm) fluted pan. Bake at 350°F (180°C) for 1 1/2 hours. Cool. Remove cake from pan and dust with powdered sugar. **Serves 8-10.**

SWEET CREAM CAKE

This cake is lovely with fresh fruit and/or Sucre à Créme. We made this often on the farm with fresh sweet cream.

2	eggs	2
⁷⁄₈ cup	whipping cream, approximately	205 mL
1 cup	sugar	250 mL
1¹⁄₂ cups	flour	375 mL
2 tsp.	baking powder	10 mL
1 tsp.	flavoring, vanilla, almond, rum, etc.	5 mL
¹⁄₂ tsp.	salt	2 mL
¹⁄₃ cup	cold water	75 mL

Put eggs into a 1 cup (250 mL) measuring cup. Fill with cream to make 1 cup (250 mL). Pour into a bowl with sugar and beat. Add flour, baking powder, flavoring and salt. Beat well. Beat in water. Pour into a greased 9" (23 cm) square pan. Bake at 350°F (180°C) for 25-30 minutes. **Serves 8-10.**

WHITE CAKE

This makes a good birthday cake.

2 cups	flour	500 mL
1 tbsp.	baking powder	15 mL
1 tsp.	salt	5 mL
³⁄₄ cup	shortening, at room temperature	175 mL
1¹⁄₂ cups	sugar	375 mL
2 tsp.	vanilla	10 mL
1 cup	milk	250 mL
5	egg whites	5

Grease and flour a 9 x 13" (23 x 33 cm) pan or 2, 9" (23 cm) layer cake pans. Combine flour, baking powder and salt. With a mixer, beat shortening, add sugar, vanilla and beat until fluffy. Add dry ingredients and milk alternately. Beat at low speed. Wash beaters and beat egg whites until stiff peaks form. Gently fold whites into flour mixture. Turn into prepared pan and bake at 350°F (180°C) for 30 minutes. Test with a toothpick to see if it's done. When cool, remove from pan. Ice with Butter Icing, page 172. **Serves 10-12.**

CRUNCHY CARAMEL CAKE

2	eggs, beaten	2
1 cup	sugar	250 mL
1 tbsp.	vanilla	15 mL
1 cup	flour	250 mL
1 tsp.	baking powder	5 mL
½ cup	milk	125 mL
¼ tsp.	salt	1 mL
3 tbsp.	butter	45 mL

TOPPING:

10 tbsp.	brown sugar	150 mL
¼ cup	melted butter or margarine	60 mL
¼ cup	whipping cream	60 mL
½ cup	shredded coconut	125 mL
1 tsp.	vanilla	5 mL

Beat eggs and sugar until light, add vanilla, flour and baking powder. Heat milk, salt and butter to boiling point. Mix into batter. Grease an 8" (20 cm) square pan. Bake at 350°F (180°C) for 30 minutes. While cake is baking, combine all topping ingredients. Remove the cake from the oven and immediately pour topping over cake. Return pan to oven and broil for 2 minutes, or until topping starts to bubble. **Serves 6-8.**

PEACH UPSIDE DOWN CAKE

A favorite for a summer picnic. This is also very good with pineapple.

⅓ cup	butter or margarine	75 mL
½ cup	brown sugar	125 mL
19 oz.	can peaches or pineapple, drained	540 mL
2	eggs	2
⅔ cup	sugar	150 mL
6 tbsp.	milk	90 mL
1 cup	flour	250 mL
3 tsp.	baking powder	15 mL
¼ tsp.	salt	1 mL

In an 8" (20 cm) square pan, melt butter or margarine. Sprinkle with brown sugar. Arrange drained peach halves or pineapple slices on butter/sugar mixture. Beat eggs and sugar, add milk. Combine dry ingredients. Add flour mixture to egg mixture, mixing well. Spread over fruit and bake at 350°F (180°C) for 45 minutes. Serve with whipped cream or ice cream. **Serves 6-8.**

HONEY CARROT CAKE

If you prefer baking with honey, this is a very good cake.

2 cups	flour	500 mL
2 tsp.	baking soda	10 mL
1/2 tsp.	allspice	2 mL
1 tsp.	cinnamon	5 mL
1/2 tsp.	salt	2 mL
4	eggs, beaten	4
1 cup	sugar	250 mL
1 cup	liquid honey	250 mL
1 cup	vegetable oil	250 mL
3 cups	grated carrots	750 mL
1 cup	raisins	250 mL
1 cup	pecans or walnuts	250 mL

Sift together flour, soda, spices and salt. Beat eggs until light. Combine sugar, liquid honey and oil and beat together with eggs. Add carrots, dry ingredients, raisins and nuts. Pour batter into 3 greased and floured 4 x 8" (10 x 20 cm) loaf pans. Bake at 325°F (160°C) for 30-40 minutes, depending on the size of your pans. Can be baked in a 9 x 13" (23 x 33 cm) pan for 40-50 minutes. Ice with Golden Butter Frosting or Caramel Frosting, page 173. **Makes 3 loaves.**

SOUR CREAM CAKE

1 cup	sour cream	250 mL
1 cup	brown sugar	250 mL
1	egg	1
1 1/2 cups	flour	375 mL
1 tsp.	baking powder	5 mL
1 tsp.	baking soda	5 mL
1/2 tsp.	cream of tartar	2 mL
1 tsp.	cinnamon	5 mL
1 tsp.	nutmeg	5 mL
1/2 tsp.	salt	2 mL
1/2 cup	raisins	125 mL
1/2 cup	walnuts	125 mL

Beat together sour cream, sugar and egg. Combine dry ingredients, raisins and nuts and add to creamed mixture. Grease and flour a 9" (23 cm) square pan. Bake at 350°F (180°C) for 30-40 minutes. Ice with Brown Sugar Frosting, page 173. **Serves 8-10.**

CHOCOLATE PINEAPPLE CARROT CAKE

Very moist — this cake uses cocoa instead of chocolate squares.

3 tbsp.	cocoa	45 mL
4 tbsp.	boiling water	60 mL
1½ cups	butter or margarine, at room temperature	375 mL
2 cups	sugar	500 mL
3	eggs, beaten	3
2 cups	grated carrots	500 mL
1 tsp.	vanilla	5 mL
1 cup	crushed pineapple with juice	250 mL
1 cup	coconut (I use Angel Flake)	250 mL
2½ cups	flour	625 mL
2 tsp.	baking soda	10 mL
1 tsp.	salt	5 mL
1 tsp.	cinnamon	5 mL
1 cup	chopped walnuts or pecans (optional)	250 mL

Dissolve cocoa in boiling water. Set aside. Cream butter, add sugar and eggs and beat until light. Add carrots, vanilla, pineapple and coconut. Mix in flour sifted with baking soda, salt, cinnamon and nuts. Add cocoa mixture last. Grease and flour a bundt pan or a 9 x 13" (23 x 33 cm) pan. Bake for 40-50 minutes at 350°F (180°C). Ice with Chocolate Icing, page 178. **Serves 8-10.**

See photograph on page 175.

EGGLESS TOMATO SOUP CAKE

This is a great cake for people who can't eat eggs.

1 cup	white sugar	250 mL
½ cup	butter or margarine	125 mL
1 tsp.	baking soda	5 mL
10 oz.	can cream of tomato soup	284 mL
2 cups	flour	500 mL
1 tsp.	cloves	5 mL
1 tsp.	cinnamon	5 mL
½ tsp.	nutmeg	2 mL
1 tsp.	baking powder	5 mL
1 cup	raisins, washed and dried	250 mL
½ cup	chopped walnuts or pecans	125 mL

Cream sugar and butter until light. Dissolve the baking soda in the tomato soup. Add to butter mixture. Sift all dry ingredients together. Add raisins,and nuts. Stir dry ingredients into the tomato soup mixture. Grease and flour a 9" (23 cm) square pan. Bake at 350°F (180°C) for 40-50 minutes. Frost with Carmel Frosting, page 173. **Serves 6-8.**

MOIST CHOCOLATE CAKE

6 tbsp.	cocoa	90 mL
1/2 cup	boiling water, or a bit more	125 mL
3/4 cup	butter or margarine	175 mL
1 1/2 cups	sugar	375 mL
4	large eggs	4
1 tsp.	vanilla	5 mL
2 1/4 cups	flour, not sifted	550 mL
1 1/2 tsp.	baking soda	7 mL
1/2 tsp.	salt	2 mL
1 1/2 cups	sour cream or buttermilk	375 mL

Mix cocoa and boiling water to a smooth paste. Add more boiling water if needed. Cool. In a large bowl, cream butter and sugar until light. Beat in 1 egg at a time. Add vanilla. Add cooled cocoa paste to the creamed mixture. Beat until well-mixed. Combine flour, baking soda and salt. Add alternately with sour cream to creamed mixture. Beat until well-mixed. Grease and flour 2, 9" (23 cm) layer cake pans. Divide batter between the 2 pans. Bake at 350°F (180°C) for 30-40 minutes. If using a 9 x 13" (23 x 33 cm) pan, bake for 50-60 minutes. Test with a wooden toothpick. When toothpick comes out clean, the cake is done. Frost with Chocolate Sour Cream Frosting, page 177. **Serves 10-12.**

See photograph on page 175.

ZUCCHINI CHOCOLATE CAKE

1/4 cup	butter or margarine	60 mL
1/2 cup	vegetable oil	125 ml
1 1/2 cups	white sugar	375 mL
2	eggs	2
1 3/4 cups	grated zucchini	425 mL
4 tbsp.	cocoa	60 mL
1 tsp.	baking powder	5 mL
1 tsp.	baking soda	5 mL
1/2 tsp.	cinnamon	2 mL
1/2 tsp.	cloves (optional)	2 mL
1 tsp.	salt	5 mL
1/2 cup	sour milk, (add 1 1/2 tsp. [7 mL] vinegar)	125 mL

2 1/4   2 1/4 cup   flour   550 mL

Beat together butter, oil, sugar and eggs, add zucchini. Sift together all dry ingredients. Mix into creamed mixture alternately with sour milk. Grease and flour a 9 x 13" (23 x 33 cm) pan. Bake at 350°F (180°C) for 45 minutes to 1 hour. Frost with Chocolate Icing, page 178. **Serves 10-12.**

HONEY CAKE

This is a Jewish honey cake and it is a very moist, very good cake.

3	eggs	3
1 cup	sugar	250 mL
1 cup	oil	250 mL
1 cup	liquid honey	250 mL
1 tsp.	baking soda	5 mL
1 cup	cold strong coffee	250 mL
3 cups	flour	750 mL
2 tsp.	baking powder	10 mL
1 tsp.	cinnamon	5 mL
½ tsp.	allspice	2 mL
½ cup	raisins	125 mL
½ cup	chopped maraschino cherries (optional)	125 mL

Beat eggs, sugar and oil until light. Beat in liquid honey. Add soda to coffee; add to batter. Add dry ingredients and mix well. Thoroughly mix in raisins and cherries, pour into greased and floured 10" (25 cm) bundt pan. Bake at 325°F (160°C) for 1 hour. Test with toothpick. You might have to bake for another 15 minutes, depending on the size of the pan. This cake keeps and freezes very well. **Serves 10.**

DARK FRUIT CAKE

3 cups	mixed candied fruit and peel	750 mL
3 cups	raisins, well-washed	750 mL
8 oz.	pkg. dates, chopped	250 g
2 cups	red and green cherries	500 mL
1 cup	slivered almonds	250 mL
1 cup	pecans	250 mL
1 cup	chopped candied pineapple	250 mL
1 cup	orange juice	250 mL
4	eggs	4
2 cups	brown sugar	500 mL
½ cup	fancy molasses	125 mL
1 cup	butter	250 mL
3 cups	flour	750 mL
2 tsp.	baking powder	10 mL
1 tsp.	salt	5 mL
2 tsp.	cinnamon	10 mL
½ tsp.	nutmeg	2 mL
½ tsp.	allspice	2 mL
½ tsp.	cloves	2 mL

DARK FRUIT CAKE

Continued

Grease brown paper and line 3, 5 x 9" (13 x 23 cm) loaf pans or use coffee cans, well-lined with the brown paper. Prepare the fruit and nuts; put in a large bowl. Pour orange juice over the fruit and let stand overnight. The next day, beat together eggs, brown sugar, molasses and butter. Sift together flour, baking powder, salt and spices and mix with the butter mixture. Add fruit to the batter; mix well. Fill pans ¾ full. Bake at 325°F (160°C) for 2 hours or more if pans are larger than 4 x 8" (10 x 20 cm). After 1 hour of baking cover the cakes with foil. Remove cakes from pan when cool. Wrap in cheesecloth that has been soaked in wine, brandy or fruit juice. Wrap in foil. Store in refrigerator for 3-4 weeks. **Makes 3 loaves.**

VARIATION: Omit molasses and add ½ cup (125 mL) of very strong cold coffee.

NOTE: To prepare cake pans, buy brown wrapping paper or use the unprinted part of a brown grocery bag. Cut brown paper the size of the pan, leaving the paper long enough so you can fold it over the batter if it starts browning too fast. Grease paper with butter. Fit paper into pans and fill ⅔ full. Use loaf pans and coffee cans.

ZUCCHINI FRUIT CAKE

This is lighter than a traditional fruit cake. Make it all year round.

3	eggs	3
1 cup	oil	250 mL
2 cups	brown sugar	500 mL
1 tsp.	vanilla	5 mL
3 cups	flour	750 mL
2 tsp.	baking soda	10 mL
½ tsp.	baking powder	2 mL
1 tsp.	each cinnamon and allspice	5 mL
½ tsp.	cloves	2 mL
1 tsp.	each nutmeg and salt	5 mL
2 cups	peeled, grated zucchini	500 mL
2 cups	raisins	500 mL
1 cup	each currants and mixed candied fruit	250 mL
1 cup	walnuts or pecans (optional)	250 mL
	brandy	

Beat eggs, add oil, sugar and vanilla. Sift together flour, baking soda, baking powder, spices and salt. Add zucchini to egg mixture, add flour mixture. Add fruits and nuts and mix well. Fill 3 greased and floured 5 x 9" (13 x 23 cm) loaf pans ⅔ full. Bake at 325°F (160°C) for 50-60 minutes. Remove cake from pans. When cold, pour brandy over cakes. Wrap and ripen for 2-3 weeks. **Makes 3 loaves.**

CREAMY CUSTARD FILLING

⅓ cup	sugar	75 mL
2 tbsp.	flour	30 mL
⅛ tsp.	salt	0.5 mL
1	egg, beaten	1
¾ cup	scalded milk	175 mL
½ cup	whipping cream, whipped	125 mL
1 tsp.	vanilla	5 mL

In a double boiler, combine sugar, flour, salt, egg and milk. Cook and stir over boiling water until thickened. Refrigerate until the custard is cold. Fold whipped cream into custard, add vanilla. Serve over a fruit salad or use as filler between layer cakes. **Makes about 2 cups (500 mL).**

BUTTER ICING

¼ cup	butter	60 mL
2 cups	icing (confectioner's) sugar, or more	500 mL
2 tbsp.	cream or milk	30 mL
1 tsp.	vanilla	5 mL
pinch	salt	pinch

Cream butter, add icing sugar, cream, vanilla and salt. Mix until smooth. You might have to add more icing sugar. Spread on cooled cake or squares. **Makes enough to frost a 9 x 13" (23 x 33 cm) cake or a double layer cake.**

VARIATIONS: For Lemon or Lime Icing, add 1 tsp. (5 mL) grated lemon or lime rind. Replace cream with 2 tbsp. (30 mL) lemon or lime juice and 1 tbsp. (15 mL) boiling water.

VANILLA GLAZE

1½ tbsp.	butter	22 mL
2 tbsp.	boiling water	30 mL
1½ cups	icing (confectioner's) sugar	375 mL
1 tsp.	vanilla	5 mL

Melt butter in boiling water, add icing sugar and vanilla. Beat until smooth. Drizzle over cakes and sweet rolls. **Makes about 1 cup (250 mL).**

GOLDEN BUTTER FROSTING

Use this for Tomato Soup Cake or a raisin or spice cake.

3 tbsp.	butter or margarine	45 mL
2 cups	sifted icing (confectioner's) sugar	500 mL
2 tbsp.	milk	30 mL
1 tsp.	vanilla or maple extract	5 mL

Heat butter in heavy saucepan until brown. Stir while heating. Remove from stove and add icing sugar, milk and vanilla. Stir until thick. Quickly spread on cake. **Makes enough to frost a 9" (23 cm) square pan.**

CARAMEL FROSTING

1 cup	brown sugar	250 mL
1/4 cup	cream	60 mL
1 tbsp.	butter	15 mL
1/2 tsp.	vanilla	2 mL

Boil all ingredients together for 3-4 minutes. When the icing starts to cool, beat until it starts to thicken. Spread on cake quickly before it gets hard. If icing gets hard before you spread it, add more cream and beat. Use for Tomato Soup Cake, page 168 or Spice cakes. **Makes about 1 cup (250 mL).**

BROWN SUGAR FROSTING

1 cup	brown sugar	250 mL
1/4 cup	cream	60 mL
3 tbsp.	butter	45 mL
1 1/2 cups	icing (confectioner's) sugar	375 mL
1 tbsp.	cream	15 mL
1 tsp.	vanilla	5 mL
1/4 tsp.	salt	1 mL

In a saucepan, combine brown sugar, 1/4 cup (60 mL) cream and butter. Cook over medium heat for 3 minutes, not more. Remove from heat and cool to lukewarm. Add icing sugar, mixing well. Stir in cream, vanilla and salt. Beat until frosting reaches spreading consistency. **Makes enough to frost a 9" (23 cm) square cake, top and sides.**

MAPLE ICING

This is a variation of Sucre à Créme. It makes a very good frosting.

4 tbsp.	butter	60 mL
3 tbsp.	cream	45 mL
⅔ cup	brown sugar	150 mL
2 cups	icing (confectioner's) sugar	500 mL
½ tsp.	maple flavoring	2 mL
½ tsp.	salt	2 mL

In a saucepan, combine butter, cream and brown sugar and bring to a boil. While hot, add remaining ingredients and beat. As you beat icing, it will get firm. Spread as soon as is starts to get thick. This icing is nice for carrot or tomato soup cake. If you prefer, use vanilla flavoring. **Makes enough to frost a 9 x 13" (23 x 33 cm) cake or a 9" (23 cm) layer cake.**

COFFEE FROSTING

2 tsp.	instant coffee	10 mL
2 tbsp.	hot water	30 mL
¼ cup	butter or margarine	60 mL
2 cups	icing (confectioner's) sugar	500 mL

Mix instant coffee and hot water. Add butter and let cool. Add icing sugar and stir until smooth. Add more icing sugar if needed. **Makes enough to ice a 9 x 13" (23 x 33 cm) cake, top and sides.**

WHIPPED CREAM FROSTING

This is a less sweet icing. It is very good.

½ tsp.	unflavored gelatin	2 mL
2 tbsp.	cold water	30 mL
1 cup	whipping cream	250 mL
¼ cup	icing (confectioner's) sugar	60 mL
½ tsp.	lemon juice	2 mL
	salt	

Sprinkle gelatin over cold water in a small bowl. Let stand to soften. Scald 2 tbsp. (30 mL) cream and pour over gelatin, stirring to dissolve. Cool. Whip cream, add confectioner's sugar, lemon juice and salt. Fold gelatin mixture into the whipped cream. Perfect for angel food or chocolate layer cakes. **Makes enough to frost a 9 x 13" (23 x 33 cm) cake.**

Chocolate & Caramel Desserts

Cheesecake with Chocolate Topping, page 159
Moist Chocolate Cake, page 169
Sucre à Créme, page 130
Café Suprême, page 48
White Chocolate Truffles, page 198
Chocolate Pineapple Carrot Cake, page 168

WHIPPED FROSTING

This is very nice for birthday cakes. It is not too sweet.

2 tbsp.	cornstarch	30 mL
1 cup	milk	250 mL
¾ cup	soft butter	175 mL
1 cup	white sugar	250 mL
1 tsp.	vanilla	5 mL
½ tsp.	salt	2 mL

In a saucepan, combine cornstarch and milk and bring to a boil; cook and stir until thick. Pour into a bowl, cover with plastic wrap and cool. In a separate bowl, beat remaining ingredients until fluffy, about 5-8 minutes. Add the cooled milk mixture; beat again for 5-8 minutes. Icing will be fluffy. **Makes enough to ice a 9 x 13" (23 x 33 cm) cake.**

VARIATION: Substitute ½ cup (125 mL) strong coffee for half of the milk to make Whipped Coffee Icing.

CHOCOLATE WHIPPED CREAM

1¼ cups	whipping cream	300 mL
¼ cup	icing (confectioner's) sugar	60 mL
½ cup	melted and cooled chocolate chips OR ¼ cup (60 mL) cocoa mixed with 3 tbsp. (45 mL) boiling water to make a paste	125 mL
1 tsp.	vanilla	5 mL

Whip cream with sugar until stiff. Add cooled chocolate mixture. Beat just to blend. Add vanilla. **Makes enough to ice a 9 x 13" (23 x 33 cm) cake.**

CHOCOLATE SOUR CREAM FROSTING

1 cup	semisweet chocolate pieces	250 mL
¼ cup	butter or margarine	60 mL
½ cup	sour cream	125 mL
¼ tsp.	salt	1 mL
1 tsp.	vanilla	5 mL
2-3 cups	icing (confectioner's) sugar	500-750 mL

Melt chocolate and butter over low heat while stirring. Cool and stir in sour cream, salt, vanilla and icing sugar. **Makes enough to ice the top and sides of 9 x 13" (23 x 33 cm) cake.**

EASY CHOCOLATE SOUR CREAM FROSTING

| 12 oz. | milk chocolate chips | 350 g |
| 2 cups | sour cream, room temperature | 500 mL |

Melt chocolate chips; mix in the sour cream. Mix well. Use to frost Moist Chocolate Cake, page 169. **Makes 2 cups (500 mL).**

See photograph on back cover.

CHOCOLATE ICING

3 tbsp.	cocoa	45 mL
2-3 tbsp.	boiling water	30-45 mL
¼ cup	butter	60 mL
1 tsp.	vanilla	5 mL
pinch	salt	pinch
2½ cups	icing (confectioner's) sugar, or more	625 mL

Mix cocoa and boiling water to make a paste. Cool. Cream butter, cocoa paste, vanilla, salt and icing sugar. Beat well. **Makes enough to ice top and sides of 9 x 13" (23 x 33 cm) cake.**

VELVET FROSTING

6 oz.	pkg. semisweet chocolate chips	170 g
½ cup	butter or margarine	125 mL
1	egg	1

Melt chocolate chips. Cool slightly. Add butter and egg. Beat until thick. **Makes enough to ice top and sides of 9 x 13" (23 x 33 cm) cake.**

NANAIMO BARS

These are truly a Canadian favorite. Since the 1950s they have been included in virtually every squares' collection.

½ cup	**butter or margarine**	125 mL
¼ cup	**white sugar**	60 mL
4 tbsp.	**cocoa**	60 mL
1	**egg**	1
2 cups	**graham wafer crumbs**	500 mL
1 cup	**coconut**	250 mL
½ cup	**chopped nuts**	125 mL
¼ cup	**butter**	60 mL
3 tbsp.	**milk**	45 mL
2 tbsp.	**Bird's vanilla custard powder**	30 mL
2 cups	**sifted icing (confectioner's) sugar**	500 mL
4 x 1 oz.	**squares semisweet chocolate, melted**	4 x 30 g
1 tbsp.	**butter**	15 mL

To make the first layer, combine ½ cup (125 mL) butter, white sugar, cocoa and egg. Cook in a double boiler, stirring until mixture resembles a custard. Add crumbs, coconut and nuts. Spread in a greased 9" (23 cm) square pan. To prepare the second layer, cream ¼ cup (60 mL) butter, milk, custard powder and icing sugar. Spread over the first layer. Melt chocolate, add 1 tbsp. (15 mL) butter. Mix well. Carefully spread over second layer or top the squares with Chocolate Icing, page 178. **Serves 10-12.**

VARIATION: For Peanut Butter Nanaimo Bars, add 2-3 tbsp. (30-45 mL) peanut butter to the custard. For Liqueur-Flavored Nanaimo Bars, replace 1-2 tbsp. (15-30 mL) of milk with Irish Crème, Amaretto, Grand Marnier or your favorite liqueur.

MARSHMALLOW SQUARES

¾ cup	butter	175 mL
½ cup	brown sugar	125 mL
1½ cups	flour	375 mL
2 tbsp.	gelatin (2 env.)	30 mL
1 cup	water	250 mL
2 cups	white sugar	500 mL
½ cup	chopped maraschino cherries	125 mL
¾ cup	toasted sliced almonds	175 mL
½ tsp.	almond flavoring	2 mL

Cream butter and sugar, add flour. Work with your hands until it is mealy. Pat into a greased 9 x 13" (23 x 33 cm) pan and bake for 25 minutes at 325°F (160°C). Cool. Soak gelatin in ½ cup (125 mL) water. Combine sugar and remaining water and boil for 3 minutes. Mix gelatin mixture with boiled sugar syrup. Beat until stiff; this takes about 8-10 minutes. To gelatin mixture, add cherries, ½ cup (125 mL) almonds and flavoring. Mix together and pour over the first layer. Sprinkle remaining almonds on top and place pan in refrigerator to cool. Cover with plastic wrap. This freezes very well. **Serves 12-14.**

LEMON CREAM CHEESE BARS

½ cup	butter	125 mL
½ cup	brown sugar	125 mL
1½ cups	flour	375 mL
1 cup	chopped almonds	250 mL
8 oz.	cream cheese	250 g
⅓ cup	white sugar	75 mL
1	egg	1
1 tbsp.	lemon rind	15 mL
1 tsp.	vanilla	5 mL
¼ tsp.	salt	1 mL
½ cup	chopped cherries (optional)	125 mL

Beat butter and brown sugar until light. Add flour and chopped almonds. Reserve ½ cup (125 mL) of this mixture for the top. Pat the rest into a greased 9" (23 cm) square pan and bake for 10-15 minutes. Let cool. Beat cheese, sugar, egg, lemon rind, vanilla and salt until light. Add chopped cherries. Spread over the bottom layer. Sprinkle with the reserved crumbs. Bake at 350°F (180°C) for 30-35 minutes. When cool, cut into squares. Cover with plastic wrap. Freezes well. **Serves 10-12.**

See photograph on page 17 and on the back cover.

ALMOND RASPBERRY SQUARES

¾ cup	butter or margarine	175 mL
¾ cup	icing (confectioner's) sugar	175 mL
2 cups	flour	500 mL
1 cup	raspberry jam, or more	250 mL
3	egg whites	3
¾ cup	sugar	175 mL
1 cup	sliced almonds	250 mL
½ cup	shredded coconut	125 mL

In a bowl, cream butter and icing sugar. Add flour and mix well. Press into a greased 9 x 13" (23 x 33 cm) pan. Bake at 350°F (180°C) for 15 minutes. Take out of oven and spread with raspberry jam. Beat egg whites until foamy. Add sugar and beat until stiff. Fold ½ cup (125 mL) of almonds into the beaten egg whites. Spread over jam. Sprinkle remaining sliced almonds on top of egg whites. Bake for 20 minutes. Slice into bars. **Serves 14-16.**

MARMALADE BARS

1 cup	flour	250 mL
¼ cup	sugar	60 mL
¼ tsp.	salt	1 mL
½ cup	butter	125 mL
½ cup	orange marmalade	125 mL
½ cup	packed brown sugar	125 mL
2	eggs	2
1 tsp.	vanilla	5 mL
1 cup	toasted hazelnuts or pecans	250 mL
1 cup	coconut	250 mL
½ tsp.	baking powder	2 mL
⅛ tsp.	salt	0.5 mL
	icing (confectioner's) sugar	

Mix together flour, sugar, salt and butter; pat into a 9" (23 cm) square pan. Bake at 350°F (180°C) for 20 minutes. Spread marmalade over crust. In a bowl, beat brown sugar and eggs until light in color. Stir in remaining ingredients, except for icing sugar. Carefully spoon egg mixture over marmalade. Bake 25 minutes. Cool and sprinkle with powdered sugar. Cut in squares or triangles. **Serves 10-12.**

CHERRY SLICE

½ cup	butter	125 mL
2 tbsp.	icing sugar	30 mL
1 cup	flour	250 mL
2	eggs, lightly beaten	2
1 cup	brown sugar	250 mL
¼ tsp.	vanilla	1 mL
¼ tsp.	almond extract	1 mL
2 tbsp.	flour	30 mL
1 tsp.	baking powder	5 mL
½ cup	chopped glazed cherries	125 mL
⅓ cup	chopped dates	75 mL
½ cup	coconut	125 mL
1 cup	chopped walnuts or pecans	250 mL

Mix together butter, icing sugar and 1 cup (250 mL) flour; spread in a greased 9" (23 cm) square pan. Bake at 325°F (160°C) for 20 minutes. Combine eggs, brown sugar, vanilla and almond extract. Mix 2 tbsp. (30 mL) flour and baking powder with fruit and nuts, add to egg mixture. Pour over first layer. Bake at 350°F (180°C) until done, 20-30 minutes. Ice with Butter Icing, page 172 and top with chopped cherries and walnuts. Freezes well. **Serves 10-12.**

See photograph on page 17.

THREE-LAYER DATE SQUARES

These date squares have a delicious brown sugar meringue topping.

⅓ cup	butter	75 mL
½ cup	brown sugar	125 mL
2	egg yolks	2
1½ cups	flour	375 mL
1 tsp.	baking powder	5 mL
¼ tsp.	salt	1 mL
1½ cups	chopped dates	375 mL
¾ cup	water	175 mL
1 tsp.	orange or lemon rind	5 mL
2	egg whites	2
¼ tsp.	salt	1 mL
1 cup	brown sugar	250 mL

THREE-LAYER DATE SQUARES

Continued

Cream butter, ½ cup (125 mL) brown sugar and egg yolks until light. Add flour, baking powder, salt and mix well. Pat into a greased 9" (23 cm) square pan. Combine dates, water and orange rind in a saucepan and bring to a boil. Cook for about 5 minutes; stirring continually. When thick stir in rind; spread over the first layer. Beat egg whites and salt until stiff. Add 1 cup (250 mL) brown sugar. Spread over the second layer and bake at 350°F (180°C) for 25-35 minutes. When cold, cut into squares and store in an air-tight container. Freezes well. **Serves 10-12.**

HINT: Always freeze squares on a cookie sheet. When they are frozen, put them in a container with waxed paper between each layer. You will find that they will hold their shape better and won't crumble easily.

See photograph on page 17.

DATE OAT SQUARES

Long ago these were called Matrimonial Squares. No plate of squares was complete without them and they are still very popular.

2 cups	flour	500 mL
2 cups	rolled oats	500 mL
¾ cup	brown sugar	175 mL
½ tsp.	baking soda	2 mL
½ tsp.	salt	2 mL
1 tsp.	vanilla	5 mL
1 cup	melted butter or ½ cup (125 mL) shortening and ½ cup (125 mL) butter	250 mL
1 lb.	dates, chopped	500 g
½ cup	white sugar	125 mL
1 cup	boiling water	250 mL
2 tsp.	lemon juice	10 mL

To prepare the first layer, in a large bowl, combine flour, oats, brown sugar, baking soda, salt, vanilla and butter. Mix thoroughly with your hands. Take a handful of mixture and give it a squeeze, if it holds together it is good, if not, add a bit more butter. Pat ⅔ of the oat mixture into a greased 9 x 13" (23 x 33 cm) pan. In a saucepan, combine dates, sugar, water and lemon juice bring to a boil and cook, stirring, for about 5 minutes, or until thick. Carefully spread date mixture over first layer. Top with remaining ⅓ of crumbs. Bake at 325°F (160°C) for about 50-60 minutes. Cut into squares. **Serves 14-16.**

See photograph on page 17.

BUTTER TART SQUARES

FIRST LAYER:

1½ cups	all-purpose flour	375 mL
½ cup	brown sugar	125 mL
½ cup	butter or margarine	125 mL
½ tsp.	salt	2 mL

SECOND LAYER:

2	eggs	2
1 cup	brown sugar	250 mL
¼ cup	white sugar	60 mL
¼ cup	melted butter	60 mL
2 tbsp.	flour	30 mL
½ tsp.	salt	2 mL
2 tbsp.	lemon juice	30 mL
1 cup	raisins or ½ cup (125 mL) each of raisins and currants	250 mL
½ cup	chopped walnuts or pecans	125 mL

Preheat oven to 350°F (180°C). To prepare first layer, blend first 4 ingredients. Work with your hands. When it's well-mixed, press lightly into a greased 9" (23 cm) square pan. Bake for 10-15 minutes. Beat eggs, brown sugar, white sugar, butter, flour and salt until light. Add lemon juice. Add raisins and nuts. Spread over first layer. Bake at 350°F (180°C) for 30-40 minutes. When cool, cut into squares. These can be iced with Butter Icing, page 172. **Serves 10-12.**

BAKING HINTS:

• You can substitute sour milk in recipes calling for buttermilk. To make sour milk, put 1 tbsp. (15 mL) of vinegar or lemon juice in a cup and fill with milk. Let stand 5 minutes before using.

• If a cake recipe calls for shortening, don't use butter or margarine. If it calls for butter, you could use margarine.

• When beating egg whites, if cream of tartar or salt is called for, first beat the egg whites until foamy, then add the cream of tartar or salt. Continue beating until the whites are stiff.

• Always preheat the oven before baking cakes, cookies or bread.

• Always use a cool cookie sheet to bake each cookie batch. This prevents the cookies from spreading too much.

CARAMEL SQUARES

½ cup	butter or margarine	125 mL
½ cup	sugar	125 mL
1	egg	1
1¼ cups	flour	300 mL
1	egg white	1
1 cup	brown sugar	250 mL
1 tsp.	vanilla	5 mL
¼ tsp.	salt	1 mL
½ cup	chopped cherries (optional)	125 mL
1 cup	chopped walnuts or pecans	250 mL

Cream together butter, sugar and egg, beating well. Stir in flour and spread in a greased 8" (20 cm) square pan. Beat egg white until stiff. Blend in brown sugar, vanilla, salt, cherries and nuts. Spread over batter and bake at 350°F (180°C) for about 30 minutes. Cut into squares. **Serves 10-12.**

WALNUT SQUARES

1 cup	flour	250 mL
½ cup	butter	125 mL
2	eggs	2
1 cup	brown sugar	250 mL
1 tsp.	flour	5 mL
½ tsp.	baking powder	2 mL
⅛ tsp.	salt	0.5 mL
1 cup	walnuts	250 mL
½ cup	coconut	125 mL

Blend flour and butter and pat into an ungreased 9" (23 cm) square pan. Bake at 350°F (180°C) for 5 minutes. Beat eggs and sugar and add remaining ingredients. Bake for 30-35 minutes. Frost when cool with Butter Icing, page 172. **Serves 10-12.**

GOOEY NUT BARS

½ cup	butter or margarine	125 mL
½ cup	brown sugar	125 mL
1½ cups	flour	375 mL
1 tsp.	baking powder	5 mL
½ cup	chopped pecans or walnuts	125 mL
2	eggs	2
¾ cup	corn syrup	175 mL
¼ cup	brown sugar	60 mL
½ tsp.	salt	2 mL
3 tbsp.	flour	45 mL
1 tsp.	vanilla	5 mL
1 cup	chopped pecans or walnuts	250 mL

Cream butter and ½ cup (125 mL) brown sugar. Add 1½ cups (375 mL) flour and baking powder. Stir in ½ cup (125 mL) chopped nuts. Pat firmly into a greased 9 x 13" (23 x 33 cm) pan. Bake at 350°F (180°C) for 10 minutes. To make the topping, beat eggs. Add syrup, ¼ cup (60 mL) brown sugar, salt, 3 tbsp. (45 mL) flour and vanilla. Add 1 cup (250 mL) chopped nuts. Pour over baked base; spread evenly; bake at 350°F (180°C) for 20-25 minutes. Don't overbake. Cut into squares while warm. **Serves 14-16.**

LEMON ALMOND BARS

1 cup	butter or margarine	250 mL
½ cup	sugar	125 mL
2¼ cups	flour	550 mL
½ tsp.	salt	2 mL
3	large eggs or 4 medium	3
1½ cups	white sugar	375 mL
⅓ cup	all-purpose flour	75 mL
1 tsp.	grated lemon rind	5 mL
½ cup	lemon juice	125 mL
1 cup	sliced almonds	250 mL

Cream butter and sugar, blend in flour and salt. Pat mixture evenly into a greased 9 x 13" (23 x 33 cm) pan. Bake at 350°F (180°C) for 20-25 minutes, until light gold. To make topping, beat eggs, sugar, flour, lemon rind and juice until light and well-mixed. Pour over baked base. Top with almonds. Bake at 350°F (180°C) for 20 minutes or a bit longer if not done. When done, filling is set and firm. Cut into bars. Freezes well. Always put waxed paper between layers of bars before freezing. **Serves 14-16.**

HONEY PECAN BARS

1¼ cups	flour	300 mL
½ cup	sugar	125 mL
½ cup	butter or margarine	125 mL
½ cup	chopped pecans	125 mL
1 cup	brown sugar	250 mL
½ cup	butter or margarine	125 mL
2	eggs	2
2 tbsp.	honey	30 mL
½ cup	chopped pecans	125 mL

Combine flour, sugar, ½ cup (125 mL) butter and ½ cup (125 mL) pecans. Pat into a greased 9" (23 cm) square pan. Bake for 20 minutes at 350°F (180°C). Meanwhile, combine brown sugar, ½ cup (125 mL) butter, eggs and honey, beat until well-mixed, add ½ cup (125 mL) pecans and mix well. Pour over hot crust; return to oven and bake for 30 minutes, or until a wooden toothpick inserted in the middle of pan comes out clean. Don't overbake. Cool and cut into bars. Ice with your favorite icing. **Serves 10-12.**

POPPY SEED POPPERS

1¾ cups	sifted flour	425 mL
1 tsp.	baking powder	5 mL
¼ tsp.	baking soda	1 mL
1¼ cups	sugar	300 mL
¼ tsp.	salt	1 mL
½ cup	melted butter	125 mL
⅓ cup	honey	75 mL
½ tsp.	almond extract	2 mL
1½ tsp.	vanilla extract	7 mL
2	eggs	2
2 tbsp.	milk	30 mL
1 cup	shredded coconut	250 mL
⅓ cup	poppy seeds	75 mL
	icing (confectioner's) sugar to decorate	

Preheat oven to 350°F (180°C) and thoroughly grease a 9 x 13" (23 x 33 cm) pan. Sift together the flour, baking powder, soda, sugar and salt. Add the butter, honey, almond and vanilla extracts, eggs and milk; mix well. Stir in coconut and poppy seeds. Pour into the pan and bake for 25 minutes. Remove from oven, place pan on wire rack, cool. Sprinkle with icing sugar and cut. **Makes about 3 dozen squares.**

FRUIT BALLS

½ cup	dried apricots	125 mL
½ cup	dates	125 mL
½ cup	seedless raisins	125 mL
1 cup	flaked coconut	250 mL
1 cup	chopped pecans	250 mL
2 tbsp.	orange juice	30 mL

Chop fruit, add ½ cup (125 mL) of coconut, chopped nuts and orange juice. Mix well. Take a teaspoonful (15 mL) of fruit and shape into a ball. Roll in the remaining coconut. Place in a container with a tight lid with waxed paper between layers. Toast the coconut if you like, it's nice both ways. **Makes about 30 balls.**

NOTE: Angel flake coconut is the type I prefer.

DATE & COCONUT BALLS

I've made this recipe for at least 50 years. These are delicious and they make good Christmas gifts.

1 tbsp.	butter	15 mL
½ cup	brown sugar	125 mL
1	egg	1
1 cup	finely chopped dates	250 mL
1 cup	chopped pecans or walnuts	250 mL
½ tsp.	vanilla	2 mL
1 cup	coconut, or more	250 mL

Cream butter, sugar and egg. Beat well. Add dates, nuts, vanilla. Drop by teaspoonfuls (5 mL) into coconut. Shape into balls and put on a greased cookie sheet. Bake at 325°F (160°C) for 20-25 minutes. These are very rich. **Makes about 24 balls.**

NOTE: All cookies should be baked on cookie sheets with no sides. The heat circulates better and the cookies bake more evenly.

PECAN PUFFS

These are an old recipe that I've made every Christmas for many years.

½ cup	butter	125 mL
3 tbsp.	sugar	45 mL
1 tsp.	vanilla	5 mL
1 cup	finely ground pecans	250 mL
1 cup	flour	250 mL
	icing (confectioner's) sugar	

In a large bowl, cream butter and sugar, beat until light. Add vanilla, ground pecans and flour, mix thoroughly. Roll dough into small balls. Place on a greased cookie sheet. Bake at 325°F (160°C) for 30-40 minutes. Bake until just golden. While hot, roll in icing sugar. Put on rack to cool. Roll again in icing sugar. When cookies are cold, store in an airtight container. **Makes about 3 dozen cookies.**

SHORTBREAD

A good shortbread recipe is a real treasure. You'll treasure this one.

1 lb.	butter	500 g
1 cup	sugar	250 mL
4-5 cups	flour	1-1.25 L
½ cup	cornstarch	125 mL
1 tsp.	salt	5 mL
	sugar	

In a large bowl, cream butter and sugar until light. Add flour, cornstarch and salt; mix well. Divide dough in half. Press into 2 ungreased 9" (23 cm) square pans. Prick with a fork all over. Bake at 325°F (160°C) for 35 minutes, until light gold. Sprinkle sugar on top and bake for another 5-10 minutes. Remove from oven and cut while hot into triangles or squares. Leave in pan until cool. **Makes about 3 dozen cookies.**

See photograph on the back cover.

BROWN SUGAR SHORTBREAD

1 cup	soft butter, or more	250 mL
¾ cup	brown sugar	175 mL
¼ tsp.	salt	1 mL
½ tsp.	vanilla	2 mL
2 cups	flour	500 mL
¼ cup	cornstarch	60 mL

Cream butter, sugar, salt and vanilla until light. Add flour and cornstarch. Mix well. If the dough is crumbly, add a bit more butter. Roll to ¼" (3 mm) thickness and cut with cookie cutter. Place on an ungreased cookie sheet. Bake at 325°F (160°C) for 20-25 minutes. These keep well and also freeze well. **Makes about 3 dozen cookies.**

ALMOND CRESCENT COOKIES

1¼ cups	flour	300 mL
½ cup	white sugar	125 mL
1½ cups	ground almonds	375 mL
1 cup	butter	250 mL
1 tsp.	vanilla	5 mL
¼ tsp.	salt	1 mL
1 cup	icing (confectioner's) sugar	250 mL

Mix flour, sugar and ground almonds. With your fingers, work in the butter, vanilla and salt until the mixture sticks together. Chill about 1 hour in the refrigerator. Roll a piece of dough between your fingers to shape a crescent. Place crescents on ungreased cookie sheet. Bake at 350°F (180°C) for 15-20 minutes, just until lightly browned. Cool for 5 minutes. While still warm, roll each cookie in icing sugar. Cool on a rack. When cold, put in a container with a tight lid. Always put waxed paper between layers of cookies when you freeze them. **Makes about 3 dozen cookies.**

NOTE: I buy ground almonds, but you can grind your own.

CHILDREN'S SUGAR COOKIES

For Christmas I decorate these cookies with colored sugar. Sprinkle the colored sugar on before baking. As a cookie cutter, I use the screw top from a quart jar. It makes big cookies. My grandchildren love them.

1 cup	butter or margarine	250 mL
1 cup	white sugar	250 mL
2	eggs	2
½ tsp.	salt	2 mL
1 tsp.	vanilla	5 mL
3 cups	all-purpose flour	750 mL
2 tsp.	baking powder	10 mL

Cream butter, sugar, eggs, salt and vanilla; beat until light. Add flour and baking powder and mix well. Roll out dough quite thin and cut with your favorite cookie cutter. Place on a greased cookie sheet. Bake at 325°F (160°C) for about 20 minutes, until just light golden brown. Don't overbake. **Makes about 3 dozen cookies.**

See photograph on the back cover.

HONEY COOKIES

This honey cookie is ideal for people who prefer to bake with honey.

1 cup	honey	250 mL
1 cup	butter	250 mL
2	eggs	2
1 tsp.	vanilla	5 mL
1 tsp.	salt	5 mL
2½ cups	flour	625 mL
3 tsp.	baking power	15 mL
1 tsp.	baking soda	5 mL

Cream honey and butter until light, add eggs and beat. Add vanilla and dry ingredients. Mix well. Drop by teaspoonful (5 mL) onto ungreased cookie sheet. Leave plenty of room for cookies to spread. Bake at 350°F (180°C) for 12-15 minutes. **Makes about 3 dozen cookies.**

JAM SANDWICH COOKIES

1 cup	butter	250 mL
pinch	salt	pinch
1 cup	brown sugar	250 mL
6 tbsp.	corn syrup	90 mL
1	egg	1
1½ tsp.	baking soda	7 mL
2½ cups	flour	625 mL
	jam	

Mix together all ingredients, except jam. Roll out dough to ⅛" (3 mm) thickness, and cut into shapes. Place on a greased cookie sheet. Bake at 350°F (180°C) for 12-15 minutes. Put together with your favorite jam, raspberry, apricot, peach, etc. **Makes about 24 double cookies.**

THUMBPRINT COOKIES

½ cup	butter	125 mL
½ cup	brown sugar	125 mL
1	egg, separated	1
1 tsp.	vanilla	5 mL
¼ tsp.	almond extract	1 mL
1 cup	flour	250 mL
pinch	baking powder	pinch
½ cup	finely chopped walnuts	125 mL
	raspberry jelly or jam	

Cream butter, sugar, egg yolk, vanilla and almond extract. Add flour, baking powder and form dough into a ball. Beat egg white with a fork until frothy but not stiff. Take a small piece of dough, roll in a ball, dip just one side in egg white, then in chopped nuts. Place on greased cookie sheet, nut side up. Press cookie center with thumb and fill the hole with your favorite jelly or jam (or half a glacéd red or green cherry). Bake at 350°F (180°C) for 20-25 minutes. Keeps well and also freezes well. **Makes about 30 cookies.**

See photograph on the back cover.

GINGERBREAD MEN

These are wonderful for Christmas gifts. You can put a small hole at the top of the head and thread with ribbons to hang on the Christmas tree.

1 cup	butter or margarine	250 mL
1 cup	packed brown sugar	250 mL
2	eggs	2
1 cup	molasses	250 mL
6 cups	flour	1.5 L
1 tbsp.	ground ginger	15 mL
2 tsp.	cinnamon	10 mL
1½ tsp.	baking soda	7 mL
1 tsp.	salt	5 mL
2 tsp.	grated orange rind	10 mL
1 tsp.	grated lemon rind	5 mL

Cream together butter, brown sugar and eggs. Beat until light. Heat molasses just until warm and add to egg mixture while stirring. Add dry ingredients and rinds. Mix well; cover with plastic wrap and let rest for an hour. On a floured counter, roll a quarter of the dough to ¼" (1 cm) thickness. Cut out gingerbread men. Place on a greased cookie sheet and bake at 350°F (180°C) for 15 minutes or more, depending on size of cookies. Repeat with remaining dough. When cold, decorate with Royal Icing. **Makes about 40 large cookies.**

See photograph on the back cover.

Royal Icing

4 cups	icing sugar	1 L
½ tsp.	cream of tartar	2 mL
3	egg whites	3

In a bowl, combine icing sugar and cream of tartar. Add egg whites and beat well. Cover with plastic wrap to keep from drying. Use piping bag to decorate gingerbread men.

VARIATIONS: Divide icing and color with food coloring as desired.

MRS. STEPHEN'S GINGER COOKIES

The chopped candied ginger gives these cookies a wonderful flavor and a chewy texture. These are soft cookies.

⅔ cup	sugar	150 mL
⅔ cup	butter or margarine	150 mL
1	egg	1
½ cup	fancy molasses	125 mL
2¼ cups	flour	550 mL
½ tsp.	ginger	2 mL
2 tsp.	baking soda	10 mL
1½ tsp.	cinnamon	7 mL
¼ tsp.	salt	1 mL
⅓ cup	milk	75 mL
1½ tsp.	vinegar	7 mL
1 cup	raisins, washed	250 mL
½ cup	chopped candied ginger (optional)	125 mL

Cream sugar and butter. Add egg, molasses and beat until light. Sift dry ingredients together. Add milk and vinegar to creamed mixture. Add dry ingredients. Add raisins and candied ginger. Mix well. Drop by teaspoonful (5 mL) onto greased cookie sheet. Bake 15-20 minutes at 350°F (180°C). These are soft cookies which keep well and freeze well. **Makes about 3 dozen cookies.**

CHOCOLATE CHIP COOKIES

This is one of my favorite chocolate chip cookie recipes.

1 cup	butter or margarine	250 mL
1 cup	dark brown sugar	250 mL
½ cup	granulated sugar	125 mL
1 tsp.	vanilla	5 mL
2	eggs, beaten	2
2½ cups	flour	625 mL
1 tsp.	baking soda	5 mL
¼ tsp.	salt	1 mL
2 cups	milk chocolate chips	500 mL
1 cup	chopped walnuts or pecans or ½ cup (125 mL) each nuts and washed raisins	250 mL

In a large bowl, cream butter, sugars and vanilla. Add beaten eggs to creamed butter; beat together. Add flour, baking soda and salt. Stir in chocolate chips and nuts or raisins. Mix well. Drop by tablespoonfuls (15 mL) on ungreased, rimless cookie sheets. Bake at 375°F (190°C) for 15-20 minutes. **Makes about 3 dozen cookies.**

NOTE: If you are allergic to nuts use raisins only.

THE BEST PEANUT BUTTER COOKIES

My daughter-in-law, Pat, gave me this recipe. With four children, the cookie jar was in constant use. It is my grandchildren's favorite cookie.

½ cup	shortening	125 mL
½ cup	peanut butter, smooth or crunchie	125 mL
½ cup	granulated sugar	125 mL
½ cup	brown sugar	125 mL
1	egg	1
½ tsp.	vanilla	2 mL
1¼ cups	all-purpose flour	300 mL
1 tsp.	baking soda	5 mL
½ tsp.	salt	2 mL

Cream together the shortening and peanut butter. Gradually beat in the sugars, egg and vanilla. Combine flour, soda and salt. Add to the creamed mixture, mixing well. Shape dough into small balls and place on greased cookie sheets. Dip a fork in water and press the cookie down. Bake at 375°F (190°C) for 15-20 minutes. These freeze well. **Makes about 2 dozen cookies.**

VARIATION: Add ½ cup (125 mL) chopped peanuts to cookie dough.

See photograph on the back cover.

SALTED PEANUT COOKIES

1 cup	flour	250 mL
1½ tsp.	baking powder	7 mL
⅓ cup	butter or margarine	75 mL
½ cup	peanut butter	125 mL
1¼ cups	brown sugar	300 mL
1	egg	1
1 tsp.	vanilla	5 mL
¼ cup	milk, just enough to make a soft dough	60 mL
1 cup	chopped salted peanuts	250 mL

Sift flour and baking powder. Cream butter, peanut butter and sugar. Add egg and beat together. Add vanilla and milk to egg mixture, then add flour mixture. Use only enough milk to make a workable dough. Shape into ¾" (2 cm) balls, roll in chopped nuts and place well apart on cookie sheet. Bake at 350°F (180°C) for 12-15 minutes. Cool on wire rack. **Makes about 2 dozen cookies.**

PEANUT BUTTER CHIP COOKIES

¾ cup	butter or margarine	175 mL
1½ cups	brown sugar	375 mL
2	eggs	2
¾ cup	peanut butter	175 mL
1½ cups	flour	375 mL
1½ cups	rolled oats	375 mL
1 tsp.	baking powder	5 mL
½ tsp.	baking soda	2 mL
1 cup	chocolate chips	250 mL
½ cup	chopped walnuts, or more	125 mL
1 tsp.	vanilla	5 mL
½ cup	milk	125 mL

Cream butter, sugar and eggs. Add the rest of the ingredients, mix well. Drop by teaspoonful (5 mL) on greased cookie sheet. Bake at 400°F (200 °C) about 20 minutes, or until light brown. **Makes about 3 dozen cookies.**

BUTTERSCOTCH CHIP COOKIES

2 cups	butterscotch chips	500 mL
½ cup	peanut butter	125 mL
2 cups	cornflakes cereal	500 mL
1 cup	Spanish peanuts	250 mL

Melt butterscotch chips and peanut butter in top of double boiler over low heat. Cool to lukewarm. Crush Corn Flakes and mix with peanuts. Add to butterscotch mixture. Drop by tablespoonful (15 mL) onto waxed paper. Keep in refrigerator or freezer. **Makes about 3 dozen cookies.**

NOTE: Make sure that you get peanuts with skins on — and not garlic flavor. This mixture hardens quickly so have paper ready and work quickly.

CANDY COOKIES

This brown sugar cookie has the added crunch of chocolate candies. Children love them.

½ cup	granulated sugar	125 mL
½ cup	brown sugar	125 mL
⅔ cup	butter, margarine or shortening	1250 mL
1 tsp.	vanilla	5 mL
1	egg	1
1½ cups	all-purpose flour	375 mL
½ tsp.	baking soda	2 mL
½ tsp.	salt	2 mL
8 oz.	M&M's candy-coated chocolate candies	250 mL

Preheat oven to 375°F (190°C). Cream sugars, butter, vanilla and egg. Add remaining ingredients. Drop dough by heaping teaspoonfuls (10 mL) about 2" (5 cm) apart onto ungreased cookie sheet. Bake until light brown but soft in the center, about 15-20 minutes. **Makes about 30 cookies.**

DROP OATMEAL COOKIES

1¼ cups	butter	300 mL
2¼ cups	brown sugar	550 mL
2	eggs	2
1 tsp.	salt	5 mL
2 tsp.	baking soda	10 mL
1½ cups	flour	375 mL
2 cups	rolled oats	500 mL
½ cup	coconut	125 mL
1 cup	dark or milk chocolate chips	250 mL
1 cup	chopped pecans or walnuts	250 mL
1 tsp.	cinnamon	5 mL
1 tsp.	vanilla	5 mL

Cream together butter and sugar, add eggs and beat until light. Add rest of ingredients. Drop by teaspoonful (5 mL) on greased cookie sheet. Bake for 15-20 minutes at 350°F (180°C). Cookies will be soft. **Makes about 4 dozen cookies.**

WHITE CHOCOLATE TRUFFLES

Apricots and amaretto make these chocolate treats absolutely mouth watering.

8	dried apricots, finely chopped	8
2 tbsp.	amaretto or other liqueur	30 mL
8 oz.	white chocolate	250 g
½ cup	finely chopped blanched almonds	125 mL
8 oz.	milk chocolate	250 g
½ cup	chocolate sprinkles	125 mL

Add chopped apricots to liqueur and let soak 30 minutes. Melt white chocolate in the oven at 250°F (120°C), watching carefully that it does not get too hot. Add to apricot mixture with almonds and mix together. Refrigerate until firm. Take a teaspoon (5 mL) of white chocolate mixture and form into small ball. Melt milk chocolate and cool. Dip balls into milk chocolate, then roll balls in chocolate sprinkles. Lay on waxed paper and store in the refrigerator. These freeze well. **Makes 24 truffles.**

See photograph on page 175 and on the back cover.

ALMOND BARK

16 oz.	white chocolate	500 g
⅔ cup	sweetened condensed milk	150 mL
2 cups	coarsely chopped toasted almonds	500 mL
½ tsp.	almond extract	2 mL

Melt white chocolate over low heat, add milk. Be careful not to overcook. Remove from heat and add almonds and extract. Spread on greased cookie sheet or waxed paper. Cool and break into pieces. **Makes about 1½ lbs. (750 g) of Almond Bark.**

PEPPERMINT BRITTLE

1 lb.	white chocolate	500 g
10	small candy canes, crushed	10
1 cup	toasted unpeeled almonds	250 mL

Heat chocolate until melted. Mix with crushed candy canes. Spread on foil-lined cookie sheet. Break into pieces when hard. **Makes about 1½ lbs. (750 g) candy.**

See photograph on the back cover.

CHOCOLATE FUDGE

⅓ cup	cocoa	75 mL
2 cups	sugar	500 mL
2 tbsp.	corn syrup	30 mL
½ tsp.	salt	2 mL
⅔ cup	cream or milk	150 mL
3 tbsp.	butter or margarine	45 mL
1 tsp.	vanilla	5 mL
1 cup	walnuts or pecans	250 mL

In a 2-quart (2 L) heavy saucepan, combine cocoa, sugar, corn syrup, salt and cream or milk. Mix and stir over medium heat until it starts to boil. Cover and let boil for 2 minutes. This will stop the crystals of sugar from sticking to the sides of the pan. Watch closely as syrup may boil over. Uncover, put in candy thermometer and boil until temperature reaches 234°F (112°C). Take off stove and do not stir. Add butter and vanilla and let syrup cool. With a wooden spoon, beat until fudge starts to thicken, add nuts and empty into a buttered 8" (20 cm) loaf pan. Cut into squares and store in a container with a tight fitting lid. Freezes very well. **Makes about 2 lbs. (1 kg).**

See photograph on the back cover.

BROWN SUGAR FUDGE

1 cup	brown sugar	250 mL
1 cup	white sugar	250 mL
¼ cup	milk or cream	60 mL
¼ tsp.	salt	1 mL
2 tbsp.	butter	30 mL
¼ tsp.	maple flavoring or vanilla	1 mL
½ cup	pecans or walnuts (optional)	125 mL

Boil sugars, milk and salt to soft ball stage, 234°F (112°C) on your candy thermometer. Remove from heat, add butter and flavoring. When cool, beat and add walnuts, if using. Pour into greased 8" (20 cm) pan. Cut into squares. **Makes about 40 squares.**

See photograph on the back cover.

ALMOND CRUNCH

1 lb.	butter	500 g
2½ cups	white sugar	625 mL
½ cup	water	125 mL
2 cups	chopped almonds, with skins on	500 mL
1 lb.	Candequick	500 g
	finely ground almonds	

Grease 2 cookie pans with sides. It's important to use a heavy pot, like a small pressure cooker or heavy Wearever pot. Melt butter over high heat, add sugar and water and mix until sugar is dissolved. Cover and boil for 3 minutes. You can't answer the phone when you make this candy! Remove lid and add nuts, stirring all the time. Mixture will start to thicken and then start to turn light gold. Keep stirring and it will start to smoke. The color of the candy should be deep gold, almost light brown. Divide candy between the cookie sheets. Spread candy quickly as it hardens fast. Set candy in a cool place. Put Candequick in oven at 275°F (140°C) in the tray that it comes with. Watch carefully. Do not overheat chocolate of any kind, it will harden. Spread Candequick on 1 side of the candy and sprinkle finely ground almonds over the chocolate. Allow to harden and repeat on other side of the candy. Candy will break, but brush the pieces with chocolate. Store in a cool dry place, don't refrigerate. **Makes about 2½ lbs. (1.25 kg) candy.**

NOTE: This is delicious candy and it makes a very good gift if you are invited out to dinner, or visiting someone during the holidays. Don't let the cost deter you. It makes a lot of first class candy. You can always find Candequick in stores around Christmas. Buy extra and put it in your freezer.

See photograph on the back cover.

PEANUT BRITTLE

This makes very nice brittle and lots of it.

3 cups	granulated sugar	750 mL
1 cup	white corn syrup	250 mL
1½ cups	water	375 mL
3 cups	raw or roasted peanuts	750 mL
1 tbsp.	baking soda	15 mL
½ cup	butter	125 mL
1 tsp.	vanilla	5 mL

Grease 2 cookie sheets. In a heavy pot, combine sugar, syrup and water. Boil until it starts to turn color. Add raw peanuts now; add roasted peanuts just as syrup turns golden. Keep stirring until syrup is medium gold. Quickly remove from stove and add soda, butter and vanilla, keep stirring. Spread as thinly as you can on prepared cookie sheets. **Makes 2½ lbs. (1.25 kg).**

HINT: You have to have a heavy pot such as a small pressure cooker or a Wearever pot. Candy will burn quickly if the pot is not heavy.

POPCORN BALLS

My niece, Annabelle Bourgoin, shared this favorite recipe with me. It is simple to make and very good. I love to try out recipes on my friends and over many years Annabelle and her husband, Maurice, have tasted and sampled many recipes for me.

1 cup	butter or margarine	250 mL
2 cups	brown sugar	500 mL
½ cup	corn syrup	125 mL
½ tsp.	salt	2 mL
½ tsp.	baking soda	2 mL
1 tsp.	vanilla	5 mL
6 qts.	popped corn (¾ cup [175 mL])	2 L

Combine butter, sugar, syrup and salt in a heavy pot. Bring to a boil, stirring constantly. Boil without stirring for 5 minutes. Remove from heat; stir in soda and vanilla. Put popcorn in a large bowl, pour warm syrup over the popcorn. Be sure it is completely coated. You could keep the popcorn warm in the oven at 250°F (120°C) while cooking the syrup. Dip hands in cold water and shape coated popcorn into balls. Wrap each ball in plastic wrap. **Makes about 36 balls.**

VARIATION: For Nutty Popcorn Balls, add 2 cups (500 mL) cashews or pecans and 2 cups (500 mL) of gum drops to above mixture.

INDEX

203

206

Share *Country Flavors* with a friend

Order *Country Flavors* at $16.95 per book plus $4.00 (total order) for shipping and handling.

Number of copies _____ x $16.95 = $ _____

Postage and handling_____ = $ _____ 4.00

Subtotal_____ = $ _____

In Canada add 7% GST_____(Subtotal x .07) = $ _____

Total enclosed _____ = $ _____

U.S. and international orders payable in U.S. funds./ Price is subject to change.

NAME:_____

STREET: _____

CITY: _____ PROV./STATE _____

COUNTRY _____ POSTAL CODE/ZIP _____

Please make cheque or money order payable to: **Bakers Trading Inc.**
(no C.O.D. orders)   **R.R. # 2**
                                                   Stony Plain, Alberta
                                                   Canada   T0E 2G0

For fund raising or volume purchases, contact **Bakers Trading Inc.** for volume rates.

Please allow 3-4 weeks for delivery

Share *Country Flavors* with a friend

Order *Country Flavors* at $16.95 per book plus $4.00 (total order) for shipping and handling.

Number of copies _____ x $16.95 = $ _____

Postage and handling_____ = $ _____ 4.00

Subtotal_____ = $ _____

In Canada add 7% GST_____(Subtotal x .07) = $ _____

Total enclosed _____ = $ _____

U.S. and international orders payable in U.S. funds./ Price is subject to change.

NAME:_____

STREET: _____

CITY: _____ PROV./STATE _____

COUNTRY _____ POSTAL CODE/ZIP _____

Please make cheque or money order payable to: **Bakers Trading Inc.**
(no C.O.D. orders)   **R.R. # 2**
                                                   Stony Plain, Alberta
                                                   Canada   T0E 2G0

For fund raising or volume purchases, contact **Bakers Trading Inc.** for volume rates.

Please allow 3-4 weeks for delivery

DO YOU NEED TO RAISE FUNDS?

Schools, Sports Clubs, Charitable & Community Groups can raise funds with *COUNTRY FLAVORS* & ENGLISH BAY FROZEN COOKIE DOUGH.

Contact Bakers Trading Inc. for Fund Raising Volume Discounts and product information.

- No investment, no risk
- Great profits

ORGANIZATION: _____

NAME: _____ TITLE: _____

STREET: _____

COUNTRY: _____ POSTAL CODE/ZIP: _____

PHONE:_____

SEND TO: BAKERS TRADING INC.
R.R. #2
Stony Plain, Alberta
Canada, T0E 2G0

DO YOU NEED TO RAISE FUNDS?

Schools, Sports Clubs, Charitable & Community Groups can raise funds with *COUNTRY FLAVORS* & ENGLISH BAY FROZEN COOKIE DOUGH.

Contact Bakers Trading Inc. for Fund Raising Volume Discounts and product information.

- No investment, no risk
- Great profits

ORGANIZATION: _____

NAME: _____ TITLE: _____

STREET: _____

COUNTRY: _____ POSTAL CODE/ZIP: _____

PHONE:_____

SEND TO: BAKERS TRADING INC.
R.R. #2
Stony Plain, Alberta
Canada, T0E 2G0